THOMAS KEITH'S SCOTLAND

JOHN HANNAVY

THOMAS KEITH'S SCOTLAND

the work of a Victorian amateur photographer

1852 – 57

Edinburgh

CANONGATE

1981

for
Marjorie Playfair-Hannay
in appreciation
of her interest and enthusiasm

V.S.W.
10-19-94
Gift of Publisher

The publishers acknowledge the financial assistance of the Scottish Arts Council
in the publication of this volume.

First published in 1981
by Canongate Publishing Limited,
17 Jeffrey Street, Edinburgh, Scotland

© John Hannavy 1981

ISBN 0 903937 73 5 cased
ISBN 0 86241 006 1 paper

Designed by Ruari McLean
Printed in Great Britain by the
Scolar Press Ilkley Ltd, Yorkshire

CONTENTS

THE PLATES

PREFACE

The publication of this book is a beginning rather than an end. In the five years since work was started, Thomas Keith has become much better known as one of Scotland's most talented Victorian amateur photographers. Examples of his work have been published throughout the world and an exhibition of his finest pictures has toured the United Kingdom.

No book is possible without the assistance of a great number of people. My special thanks are due to Marjorie Playfair-Hannay, who provided the original inspiration, and to my wife Eileen, who has followed up many of the leads.

I am particularly grateful to the members of the Scottish Photography Group who presented the touring exhibition of Keith's work, and especially to Richard Hough for his painstaking efforts to ensure optimum quality in the modern prints from which the plates in this book are produced.

To the City Librarians and the Staff of Edinburgh Central Library over the past five years who have answered countless queries and letters, and to Helmut Gernsheim who placed much valuable information at my disposal, I also owe a debt of gratitude.

My thanks also to John Ward of the Science Museum, London; Joe Coltharp of the Gernsheim Collection, University of Texas; Ian Smith of the Edinburgh Photographic Society; Robert Sobieszek of the International Museum of Photography, New York; Andre Jammes in Paris; Professor J. Chassar Moir; The Scots Ancestry Research Society; The Royal Scottish Academy; The Scottish National Portrait Gallery; the Iona Cathedral Trust; the Royal College of Surgeons, Edinburgh; the Victoria and Albert Museum, London; the British Library; Brian Coe of the Kodak Museum; Mrs Dorothy Schultze and many others to all of whom I am very grateful.

John Hannavy, Wigan, 1980

IN – TEXT ILLUSTRATIONS

INTRODUCTION

A colleague once told me that the greatest satisfaction in his work was the thrill of discovery – that superb moment when the researcher, having carefully followed up obscure references and leads, discovers something new or finds answer to a long-standing question. If that is true of those involved in photographic history, then Thomas Keith has been responsible for a great deal of pleasure. His photographs have been 'discovered' a number of times but little has been done with the fruits of those discoveries until now.

I too discovered Keith almost by accident, having been asked to make a series of prints from some paper negatives lent to me by a friend. These negatives, measuring about 25cm × 28cm, photographer unknown, and showing scenes of Edinburgh and Central Scotland, had come to me because several others had been reluctant to print them. Initially they were of interest to their owner simply for the hidden locations and subjects which such prints would reveal. Once the negatives had been dated – a relatively simple task after reference to Edinburgh building records – it was possible to deduce that they were the work of Thomas Keith by comparison with known Keith negatives and in consideration of his unique style. In the course of a great deal of reading after the initial discovery had been made, I found I was merely the latest in a long line of people to 'discover' this unique talent.

Sixty years before me, Alvin Langdon Coburn, himself now a respected figure in the history of photography, wrote these lines:

> 'I was having tea one afternoon in a street near the British Museum with a friend who is wise in book-lore when we were joined in our corner by a tall acquaintance of his, and the talk turned, as often happens to do when I am in the company, to the work of [David Octavius] Hill. "But" said the newcomer, "do you know of the photographs of Dr Keith?"
>
> At once I was all attention for he looked the sort of man who uttered truths. No, I did not know of the work of Dr Keith. Then I was told that his photographs were "as good as Hill's" and I lost no time in writing to Dr Keith's family to inquire if I might by any chance be permitted to look over such pictures as they possessed.
>
> I received in reply a most kind letter asking me to call on a certain afternoon and imagine my joy when the Misses Keith spread before me not only several large volumes of beautiful prints, but also negatives! They were paper negatives.......and the prints I made from them were shown at the Exhibition of the

Royal Photographic Society last year [1914]. To the best of my knowledge and belief, these were the first things of Dr Keith's to be publicly shown.'[1]

While Coburn's claim to be the first to exhibit Keith's work (after his death) appears to be correct, he was by no means the first to appreciate his talent. Even in his own lifetime Keith was being classed as one of the most important figures in the history of the paper negative. In 1885, ten years before his death, John Gray wrote:

> 'Many calotypes of quite exceptional beauty and artistic quality were executed by Dr Thomas Keith between the years 1850 and 1855.'[2]

The dates are interesting, 1850 being at least a year earlier than Keith's first datable image and 1855 some years before a number of his finest photographs. Also, his works were clearly not 'calotypes'.

Thomas Keith was 'discovered' again in the 1950's by Neven du Mont who wrote that Keith's work was:

> 'Unique not only for its quality but because it has only recently been discovered'.[3]

Discovering Thomas Keith is a formidable experience. The salted paper prints may be a little faded in many cases – although some of the surviving albums contain exquisite examples – but the negatives are a photographic treasure indeed. Their quality denies their great age and their printing characteristics suggest that those of us working in photography today have much to learn about subtlety and technique.

More important however than mere technical consideration, is the sheer brilliance of Dr Keith's picture-making. Here, perhaps for the first time — practical photography was about twelve years old when Keith first experimented — is an amateur who is not satisfied by the mere journey through a sequence of technical steps – a journey which leads to a photograph for its own sake. Too many photographers at the time felt that the mere fact of having successfully taken a picture made the end product worthwhile. Keith, with the eye of the artist, brought to amateur photography its first real master, using the vast potential of mid-Victorian Edinburgh as the subject for a series of compositions in line, texture, and shape, making a definite statement and not just a series of records.

We hope that the latest 'discovery' of Thomas Keith's photography will survive. It is the hope of every historian that his discovery will reach a wide and appreciative public. Doubtless that was Du Mont's hope, and that of Coburn before him. This time, thanks to the Scottish Photography Group, I have been able to develop my ideas of Keith's photography more fully. Fifty-five examples of Keith's photography formed the basis of an exhibition which opened at the Group's 'Stills' gallery in Edinburgh in early summer 1977. In 1978 it toured the country. The illustrations for this book include many pictures from that exhibition. The pictures are a testament to the genius of Dr Thomas Keith.

An engraved portrait of Thomas Keith bearing his own signature. There is no information available on this portrait except the obvious one of subject.

The fact that it is genuinely Keith's signature – clearly part of the printed image and not handwritten on the print itself – suggests that this might be a self-portrait (although this is unlikely).

The signature was authenticated with the recent discovery of some letters from Dr Keith to his patients from the 1870's.

Reproduced by permission of Edinburgh City Libraries.

CHAPTER 1

To be alive in the first half of the last century was to live through a period of achievement and discovery in science and technology.

Thomas Keith and photography were born within two months of each other – Keith in May 1827 and photography, in the form of the heliograph invented by Joseph Nicéphore Niepce in France, in July of the same year. Although that early process proved to be somewhat of a dead end, a quarter of a century later the infant art had matured to a degree where considerable success could be achieved in the hands of the talented photographer.

Keith was born in the little village of St Cyrus in Kincardineshire and, to look at the history of the family after Thomas's day, it would be easy to conclude that it had a medical tradition. But before Thomas was born, the strongest tradition was with the Church. He was one of seven sons born to the Minister of the Church of Scotland in the village, the Reverend Alexander Keith, who had followed his father into the ministry. He in turn would be followed by one of his sons, Alexander Secundus. But Thomas and four of his brothers entered the medical profession, as did two of Thomas's own sons and least one of his daughters. Much of the basic information contained in standard medical texts written by his sons the year before his death can be traced to Thomas's medical research.

Thomas's education followed a very typical pattern – parish school followed by Aberdeen Grammar School and three years studying art at Aberdeen's Marischal College. This early association with the arts would be put to very good use in his later photographic days.

In 1845 he was apprenticed to Sir James Young Simpson at Edinburgh's Old Infirmary and was, as far as records show, the last medical apprentice in the city. Until then it had been relatively common practice for young men to enter medicine by 'serving their time'. After 1845 the traditional system of full-time training, more in line with today's university courses, was adopted.

For the young Thomas Keith however this apprenticeship was to prove most valuable, working as he did for a much respected surgeon and great medical pioneer. Simpson, one of Scotland's leading gynaecologists, and his team (which included Thomas's elder brother George Skene Keith) were involved in research in anaesthesia. Work in this field had been going on for over forty years since 1799, when Humphrey Davy (of safety lamp fame and himself an early photographic pioneer with Thomas Wedgewood) had discovered the properties of nitrous oxide (laughing gas) as an anaesthetic and local pain reliever. Michael Faraday had later shown that ether had

1 The Reverend Dr Alexander Keith, Thomas Keith's father, photographed by D. O. Hill and Robert Adamson as a preliminary study for the Disruption Painting. This photographic session, probably in Edinburgh, may have been Thomas Keith's first close contact with the intricacies of the new art. *Scottish National Portrait Gallery.*

similar properties and as early as 1842 an operation under ether had been conducted by Dr Crawford Long in America. Simpson's initial interest appears to have been the alleviation of distress during childbirth and his first deliveries under ether were carried out in 1847.

At almost exactly the same time as Simpson was performing his first anaesthetised operations in Scotland, a paper was being read by M. J. Flourens to the Académie des Sciences in Paris on the effect of chloroform on animals. Simpson and his team were quick to see the implications of this paper and their first operation under chloroform was carried out in Edinburgh in November 1847. Although George Skene Keith was Simpson's assistant during these experiments and operations, Thomas, as a junior member of the team, was present and able to learn from his 'master's' discoveries.

On qualifying in the following year, 1848, Keith was appointed house surgeon to James Syme at Edinburgh Infirmary. Syme was at the time one of Scotland's leading

2 Portrait of Dr Thomas Keith late in life. (From a painting.) *Royal College of Surgeons, Edinburgh.*

consultants and Keith's appointment no doubt reflected Simpson's opinion of his apprentice. Thomas originally intended to hold this appointment for at least two years but in the autumn of the following year, at the age of only twenty-two, he was offered, and accepted, the position of house surgeon to the British Embassy at the Court of the King of Sardinia in Turin. (There is, surprisingly, no official record of this appointment, and so we can only assume that it was of a private nature rather than an embassy appointment.)

Two years later he returned to Edinburgh and resumed his work with Syme, sharing the latter's desire to see considerable reforms in medical practice in Scotland. Thomas returned to Scotland via London and, being in that city at the time of the Great Exhibition in Hyde Park, it would be surprising if he had not been drawn to that great advertisement of British achievement.

After a further two years with Syme, Thomas eventually left the Infirmary in 1853 to join his brother's general practice. He was replaced by a young doctor, Joseph Lister, another of Scotland's great medical pioneers, and the two men became great friends and colleagues throughout the remainder of their medical careers. A decade later Lister rose to international fame as the pioneer of antiseptic surgery, and their joint belief in the importance of absolute cleanliness in the operating theatre was the key to their professional friendship and their medical success. It is ironic that it was Lister's carbolic spray, used to sterilise the operating theatre and the medical instruments, which aggravated a lifelong illness to a point where Thomas suffered almost constant pain and frequent haemorrhages in later life. It was typical of the man that the safety of his patients was of infinitely greater importance than his own health. (Before the introduction of the spray in the 1880's, he had sterilised all his instruments with a spirit lamp, but believed Lister's carbolic spray to be more efficient.)

In his first few months with Syme at Edinburgh Infirmary, Thomas Keith had become recognised as a specialist in complaints of the ear, although his first love was always surgery. Therefore when he and George Skene Keith set up their private practice, their work included surgery in addition to general medical work. In the 1870's, dissatisfied with the conditions in the new Edinburgh Infirmary, Thomas and George opened their own private infirmary in Great Stuart Street where all their beliefs on cleanliness were put into daily use. Although this was a private infirmary, Thomas and George Skene Keith followed the example set by Syme years before at his Minto House hospital of mixing both fee-paying private patients and charity work for the large numbers of poor people in the city.

Once away from the Infirmary, Thomas found himself drawn more and more towards surgery, and more particularly towards gynaecology, specialising in and pioneering ovarian surgery. All these developments in his medical career however postdate the period with which this book is particularly concerned – the five or six years during which Thomas Keith turned to photography as a hobby.

In one of several obituaries of Thomas Keith there is a short quote which serves both as an end to this brief sketch of his early medical work, and as an introduction to his involvement with photography:

"Keith was always in earnest; and whatever he found to do, he did it with all his might."

CHAPTER 2

The Britain to which Thomas Keith returned from Turin in the autumn of 1851 was very different from the country he had left. He returned to the London of the Great Exhibition, with crowds of over 40,000 people a day trouping to Joseph Paxton's Crystal Palace in Hyde Park to see the marvels of the modern world. The Great Exhibition was only a dream when he left but by the time of his return it had been open for three months and had already attracted between three and four million visitors. It was a sudden blossoming of British confidence in her new technology and the lavishly-produced catalogues, in several volumes, gave full coverage of the breadth of British achievement and ingenuity.

The new art of photography was of course included, although many people were distressed to find it amongst the sciences and engineering and not amongst the arts, where they felt it ought to be. Henry Fox Talbot, the father of modern photography, had used his calotype process to record the prizewinning entries in each section and the bound 'Reports of the Juries' contained many fine photographs.

The exhibition – 'The Great Exhibition of the World's Industry' and the brainchild of Prince Albert — opened at a time when *practical* photography, based on the process pioneered by Talbot, was only eleven years old and was still very much a novelty. A short history of the 'new art' was published in the exhibition catalogue.

'The discovery of this beautiful application of the chemical properties of light is of very recent date. Efforts to fix the illuminated images by means of the chemical agency were made by Wedgewood and Davy as early as 1802, but without success, no preparations being discovered sufficiently sensitive to be affected by the subdued light of the camera. Sir H. Davy obtained a faint impression of the illuminated image produced in a solar microscope; but being unacquainted with any method of suspending the further action of light on the picture, no permanently perfect effect resulted, and the subject was laid aside. In the fourteen years which elapsed between 1814 and 1828, the labours of M. Daguerre and M. Niepce were directed to the solution of the problem. In 1827 a memoir was presented by the latter to the Royal Society, accompanied by several specimens of *Heliographs – sun drawn* pictures. These, which are still extant, show that M. Niepce was acquainted with a method of forming pictures, by which the lights and shadows are represented as in nature, and when so formed, of

rendering proof against the further effects of light. M. Niepce, however, having concealed his process, describing only the results, the Society could not, according to its rules, admit his memoir to the transactions. The surfaces upon which he produced his pictures were those of glass, copper plated with silver, and well polished tin. Those upon which M. Daguerre produced his first pictures were impregnated with nitrate of silver. About six months before the disclosures of the processes of Daguerre and Niepce, Mr Fox Talbot read before the Royal Society a memoir, in which he explained his photographic researches, and showed the manner in which he produced upon paper, rendered sensitive by chemical preparation, photographic pictures.

This report, perhaps one of the first accounts of the invention of photography, is highly inaccurate. It attributes to Niepce the invention of the Daguerreotype process while ignoring Niepce's early successful experiment in 1827 on pewter plates, which survives today as the earliest known photograph. The Niepce process involved a pewter plate coated with bitumen of Judea which, after eight hours exposure, hardened to give a direct positive image of very coarse grain and poor definition. However it remains the first successful method of producing a photographic image in a camera. The original is in the Gernsheim Collection, University of Texas at Austin. Several dates have been given for this image, but recent researches have suggested July 1827 as the date of public announcement — perhaps dating the photograph just a few weeks earlier. The Daguerreotype, announced in 1839, was the result of extensive research and cooperation between Daguerre and Niepce. The process used a silvered copper plate, sensitised with chlorine and iodine vapours and developed over mercury vapour. The photograph, a direct positive, was unique, and copies could only be made by re-photographing the original.

It is interesting that the daguerreotype should have been chosen for Alexander Keith's second expedition to get accurate illustrations for his book. It was a complex process, yielding only a single positive image as opposed to the more versatile negative of the calotype. The daguerreotype did however have the advantage of usually employing a smaller camera, thus reducing the total weight of equipment to be carried – an important consideration on a long and difficult journey as Alexander must have found out the hard way the previous year. Just where George learned the process is unknown but he was clearly competent as the engravings based on his work show.

The early photographic influences on Thomas's life were continued when he joined his brother in Edinburgh – George's hobby coinciding with the first years of Thomas's medical apprenticeship.

The Great Exhibition of 1851 is bound to have rekindled this early interest in photography after his return from Turin. But Thomas must have been aware that his potential as a photographer was restricted not only by the rigours of his medical commitments, but also by the limitations of the processes currently available. His brother's free time must have been just as limited as his, and Thomas could not have ignored the obvious problems of manipulating the daguerreotype process under such restricting conditions. His choice of a paper process over either silvered copper (daguerreotype) or the recently introduced glass (wet collodion) processes was for entirely sound reasons.

To him photography was essentially a hobby, to be pursued only after the day's medical work was at an end. It had therefore to fit into his daily timetable, allowing for all the chemical preparations to be undertaken and the photographs themselves to be taken at the beginning and the end of each day. From his own account of his photography, we read:

> 'I sensitize my paper overnight, for in the middle of summer I am almost always sure of clear mornings soon after sunrise, and most of my negatives have been taken before 7 in the morning, or after 4 in the afternoon. The light then is much softer, the shadows are larger and the halftints in your pictures are more perfect, and the lights more agreeable.'[1]

With these restrictions on his time, only a process which allowed the bulk of its preparation to be completed the night before would be of any use to Keith. None of the other processes really offered him this facility. The calotype was however a little crude at times, and it was a second paper process, the Waxed Paper Process pioneered by the Frenchman Gustavele Gray, which Keith adopted. The differences between the two paper processes – subtle but immensely important, are more fully detailed at the end of this book.[2] Suffice to say at this stage that the waxed paper process was capable of finer detail and, therefore better quality.

The albumen-on-glass process was too slow and, with glass plates to carry around, too heavy. The daguerreotype, by the early 1850's was already on the way out of favour in Europe – although its success in America continued for almost a further decade. Wet collodion, also based on glass, had similar weight drawbacks – together with the problem of the photographer having to carry a darkroom around with him to prepare his plates.

Thomas Keith would no doubt already be familiar with the material 'collodion' before Frederick Scott Archer published his account of the wet collodion process in *The Chemist* in March 1851. Collodion, a mixture of guncotton and ether, had been the subject of a series of experiments by Simpson in 1848. He was probably one of the first people in Britain to apply collodion to the dressing of wounds after surgery. (Collodion when dried formed a clear, thin and airtight film, ideal for the purpose). An application of this material in surgery had been proposed the year before in America.

Archer's original idea of applying the material to photography had been to use the film properties of collodion as a replacement for the opaque paper base of the calotype. However, he found that when the sensitised material dried the exposure times required in the camera were too long. The final practical version of the process required the photographer to coat his glass plate with an even layer of wet collodion which was subsequently sensitised and exposed wet. This innovation, while greatly increasing the 'speed' of the process, also considerably increased its inconvenience. But only waxed paper gave the photographer the combination of high image quality with the facility of being able to pick up a small amount of equipment (by Victorian photographic standards) and go out whenever the weather was suitable.

There is no doubt that the wet collodion process did give finer quality negatives – being on glass they were clearer and brighter. That meant that prints could be made from them more easily – a strong point in the process's favour from the professional's point of view. To them the bulk of a portable dark-tent, darkroom or mobile photographic van was a slight inconvenience if they produced negatives which could be printed at the rate of several per day. (Printing in these times was by contact in sunlight. A wet collodion negative could be printed in about one fifth of the time required for even a waxed paper negative). For the amateur those trappings were the only drawback to an otherwise ideal process. While for the professional, printing time was essential – with upwards of a hundred prints being made from each negative for sale through print shops across the country – the amateur's prime consideration was actual camera time.

While Thomas Keith could sensitize and prepare his papers the night before a day's photography, the wet plate photographer had to coat his glass plates immediately before exposing them in the camera and then develop and fix them before the sticky emulsion dried. With daylight at a premium few amateurs initially took up such a laborious process. The professional drawback of the paper process – printing time – was of little consequence to the amateur, as there was ample daylight of the wrong quality for actual photography which could be devoted to making prints from already processed negatives. As the average amateur made only two or three prints from each negative, such restrictions were unimportant.

For Thomas Keith, the major attraction of the waxed paper process was the simple fact that his negative papers, once coated, dried and loaded into his darkslides, could be stored unexposed if necessary for several days, until he had sufficient time to indulge in his hobby.

> 'Last summer for instance, I had prepared half a dozen pieces of paper, but on account of the very wet weather had no opportunity of using them for six days afterwards. Three of them had been put into the slides immediately after being blotted off. These when developed turned out excellent negatives.'[3]

With collodion, a few minutes rather than a few days was

the maximum storage time possible. (The ether which formed the basis of the collodion evaporated quickly, lowering the sensitivity of the plates.)

It should be pointed out – as Dr Keith did in his published accounts – that this practice of keeping slides for several days was the exception rather than the rule. By limiting his photography to a few weeks in the summer, he reduced the possibility of encountering bad weather. During those weeks it was not too much trouble to carry even a few loaded slides and his lightweight camera into the hospital with him, either after an early morning photographic excursion or in anticipation of an early evening expedition. Keith lived very close to his work and so, even if he had to return home to collect his equipment, only a few minutes of valuable light would be lost if all the preparations were completed the night before. The cameras he used were probably folding bellows cameras – of large format but designed for easy transportation. Thus, with only a few pounds of equipment to carry, he was able to walk extensively around the old city in search of new pictures.

It is not certain just when he took his first photograph – certainly the often-quoted date of 1854 is much too late. True, his earliest dated pictures bear that date, but it is much more likely that 1852 at the latest marked the beginnings of this new hobby. In his paper to the Photographic Society of Scotland in 1856, and which we include in full as an appendix to this book,[4] he states quite clearly that 'two or three years ago' he was producing pictures which entirely satisfied him:

'The best paper I ever had was some of Canson's thin negative, which I got from Sandford about three years ago. I have not been able since then to procure any of a similar quality. Turner's and Whitman's papers give excellent results, but the washing of English papers is very difficult, and therefore the thin French paper is preferable.'*

Likewise the report attributes to Daguerre the invention of photography on paper, today associated with Fox Talbot. Talbot's Calotype or Talbotype process succeeded his earlier Photogenic Drawing Process (c.1835) and was announced early in 1840, being patented the following year. The paper negative was of coarser quality than the daguerreotype, but the facility to print multiple copies was Talbot's considerable achievement in the evolution of photography. With the introduction of the calotype, words

such as 'negative' 'positive' and 'development' became common photographic terms.

It continued however in more accurate vein to describe the basic principles of photography:

'The vast number of beautiful sun-drawn pictures on various sorts of surfaces which are presented in the exhibition demonstrate how great and how rapid has been the progress of the art from the date of its invention. The results are invariably denominated either from the names of their inventor or discoverer, as Daguerreotype and Talbotype, or from the principle by which the surface destined to receive the picture is rendered sensitive to light – as cyanotype, chrysotype, chromotype. Pictures produced by the photographic process are of two types; first positive pictures in which the lights and shades correspond with the object represented; the second, negative pictures in which the lights and shades are reversed, the lights being represented by shadows, and the shadows by light. In the Talbotype process, as it is sometimes called, the picture being produced in the camera is usually negative. This picture being laid upon another sheet of paper coated with chloride of silver, and then exposed in sunshine, a positive picture, corresponding exactly with the negative one is obtained.'

It is interesting, in a world where photography is considered essential to almost every aspect of modern life, to imagine that initial public reaction to such a new and seemingly magical way of making pictures. The impact of the Great Exhibition would have served only to renew in Thomas Keith an already established interest in photography.

The Keith family had shown interest in the calotype process within the first few months after Talbot's announcement and patent in 1841. But the family's first real encounter with the process came with the 'Disruption' in 1843 when Dr Alexander Keith, Thomas's father, became one of the Ministers to leave the Church of Scotland with Thomas Chalmers and form the Free Church of Scotland. David Octavius Hill's decision to paint a huge canvas to commemorate the event and to do so using photographs as an aid to the mammoth task, brought Alexander Keith in front of the camera lens for the first time. (Hill was originally intending to record the first meeting of the Free Church of Scotland, but later changed his mind and based the painting on the Signing of the Deed of Demission at Tanfield a few weeks later. Both Hill and Adamson themselves appear in the painting which took over a decade to complete.) Thomas's brother, Alexander Secundus, also posed for Hill and Adamson, probably in late 1843. That date is unproven, but it is the only possible time for the sitting, as Dr Keith Senior left Scotland early in 1844 on a visit to Palestine. Neither he nor his son would have been particularly pleased to read early in 1844 in the *Quarterly Review* that Hill and Adamson were photographing the 'fat

---

* Already, within a little over a decade of the introduction of photography on paper, several companies were producing papers especially for photography. After his initial success with Canson paper, Keith eventually settled for Rive paper, another thin French variety. Whatman paper, mentioned in the extract, was the frequent choice of Hill and Adamson. Whatman's Turkey Mill, however, was a heavily water-marked paper and this often made for complications in selecting pieces suitable for use as photographic negatives. Several of Hill and Adamson's pictures are marred by the intrusion of the watermark.

3 Keith must also have been influenced by his brother George's daguerreotypes in connection with their father's travels in Palestine and Syria, ultimately used as the basis of engravings in *Evidence of the Truth of the Christian Religion*.

Martyrs of the Free Kirk'.

The impact of that brief encounter with Hill and Adamson on Dr Keith was considerable. In the few months between the sitting and his departure for the Holy Land someone – presumably Adamson – instructed him on the intricacies of the calotype process and equipped him with the usual paraphenalia of the travelling photographer.

That visit – his second – did result in some pictures, but he was clearly dissatisfied with the results. Perhaps it was the unsuitability of the process for the conditions in which he was working, or the speed of his education in the procedures of photography which let him down, but he resolved to return in the following year, 1845, with his son George, a keen amateur daguerreotypist. The resulting pictures from that third visit were used as a basis for engravings in one of the later editions of Alexander Keith's *Evidence of the Truth of the Christian Religion*, originally

published in 1837 and eventually produced in over forty editions and several languages.

Thomas, a young man in his teens, cannot have failed to become interested in this wealth of photographic experimentation. His father's unsuccessful efforts with the calotype, Hill and Adamson's clearly successful work with the same process, and then George's successes with the French daguerreotype process must all have fascinated him. In this variety of processes around him Thomas must surely have been increasingly aware of the potential of each.

Now, if 'three years ago' he was producing excellent results, and the paper was written early in 1856, then he was producing images of a quality acceptable to his high personal standards as early as 1853. We can therefore reasonably submit that his initial experiments must have been made in 1852 at the latest. There is evidence in some of what this writer assumes to be Keith's earliest negatives that such early experiments were made before Keith's self-imposed rules about limiting his photography to mid-summer and early autumn. In some views (including an early and rare pair of stereoscopic negatives) there is what appears to be snow on the ground – suggesting perhaps that the winter of 1851/52 and the summer of 1852 were used to iron out initial problems with the manipulation of the process. These dates would tie in with the idea that the Great Exhibition, immediately upon his return from Italy, acted as the stimulus to this new interest. Certainly to modify and experiment with the waxed paper process to a level where it entirely suited his requirements would take at least a few months of careful work.

At this time Dr Keith was living at 58 Northumberland Street in Edinburgh's New Town, and there exists what is presumably a very early experimental negative showing the back elevation of this house. This and perhaps other views (since lost) of his home, were followed by an extensive series of pictures in Greyfriar's Churchyard. This was the site of Hill and Adamson's early experimental work, and a location ideally suited for photography. The ornate tombs and the over-grown ruin of the ancient church (since restored) provided a truly romantic setting for many of Edinburgh's pioneer photographers.

Keith's photography however appears from the outset to have involved more than the simple wish to produce romantic compositions. His pictures of the churchyard so closely echo Hill's that the obvious conclusion is of intention rather than accident. Keith used figures sparingly in these pictures but, where they do appear, their pose and position resembles Hill's earlier work. Perhaps Keith was experiencing the basic problems of photography – composition, manipulation of the camera, posing figures in such a way that they could remain still for the long exposures, and so on – in such a way that he could relate his findings to the already accepted standards of achievement of his friend and – perhaps – his teacher.

As a relief from the pressures of medicine, photography seemed the perfect hobby for Thomas Keith. Always a perfectionist, he would not have wished even his hobby to have asked less of him. Only the tensions were different – the standards of technique and care which he applied to medicine and photography were the same. To Thomas Keith, everything seems to have been viewed in terms of the challenge it presented. It was this same challenging spirit which led to completely new heights of achievement during his long and eminent medical career.

In 1854, the year of his earliest dated picture, a new interest came into his life when, on 4 June, he married Elizabeth Johnston, whose first cousin was the wife of Keith's friend and mentor, Sir James Young Simpson. Thomas's father conducted the ceremony and the couple left on their honeymoon in Braemar. That expedition marks the beginnings of Thomas's true understanding of the medium of photography – the pictures he took during these two weeks, using trees as subjects, are the earliest known successful examples of his work.

Further evidence of the standard of his photography by 1854 comes from the account of Edinburgh's first photographic exhibition – held in March – when Keith's work appeared alongside that of Hill and Adamson, Gustave le Gray himself, and George Washington Wilson of Aberdeen (who was to become one of Scotland's leading professional photographers and Photographer Royal to Queen Victoria in Scotland).

Surely, if Keith himself was prepared to exhibit his work in such illustrious company, more than just elementary experiments had been conducted in the previous summer. Unfortunately the account of the exhibition gives us no insight into the particular images which were exhibited, but it is further evidence to support an earlier introduction to the waxed paper process.

4 The back of 58 Northumberland Street, Edinburgh – presumably a very early experiment with the waxed paper process. Keith lived at this address for several years, and during most of his association with photography. *Edinburgh City Libraries.*

5 The Castle from Greyfriars by Hill and Adamson. *Scottish National Portrait Gallery*.

7 Tomb of Sir Robert Dennystoun, by Hill and Adamson. *Scottish National Portrait Gallery*.

6 The Castle from Greyfriars by Thomas Keith. The camera positions are remarkably similar. Where Hill and Adamson incorporated figures, Keith has relied on the strong shapes and patterns of the ivy which has covered the walls in the intervening years. *Edinburgh City Libraries*.

8 Tomb of Sir Robert Dennystoun, by Thomas Keith. Here Keith has echoed Hill and Adamson even further with the inclusion of a seated figure. However Keith's figure is less crucial to the overall success of the picture than Hill and Adamson's. While the figures are the central factor in the earlier image, Keith is already using lighting and camera angle to produce a more descriptive account of the place itself. *Edinburgh City Libraries*.

Figs 5–10
The close comparisons between Hill and Adamson's work and Keith's early experiments do more than just suggest a link. There can be little doubt that in these photographs Keith is simply imitating two established masters of photography for whom he doubtless had considerable respect. The opportunity to repeat absolutely each experimental image, coupled with the romantic potential of this delightfully overgrown churchyard, made it an obvious choice for his early work. The fact that he could also copy the work of Hill and Adamson, and thus experience many of the problems which they must clearly have experienced, would have made the exercise doubly beneficial.

9 Tomb of John Cunninghame, by Hill and Adamson. *Scottish National Portrait Gallery.*

11 Tomb of John Naysmythe, Greyfriars. Here the personal interpretation of Thomas Keith is given full rein. The approach is totally direct, the figures are gone and the image relies for its success solely on the lighting conditions and the framing of the subject. The picture, at first unspectacular and yet attractive, involves the viewer more and more – the small skull peering through the heavy gloom of the foliage, the mysterious blackness of the tomb, the strong angular shapes, all combine to produce a fascinating study. *Edinburgh City Libraries.*

10 Tomb of John Cunninghame, by Thomas Keith. Still using Hill's idea of a seated figure, Keith's own personal style continues to emerge. In the Hill/Adamson image, the figure is again surrounded by, but not really a part of, the remainder of the picture. In the Keith version the slightly different location of the figure gives him a purpose within the composition – as an aid to scale – dwarfed as he is by the massive monument. Again, the personal touch can be perceived in the more direct approach of Keith to the tombs. The slightly oblique, more distant view of Hill and Adamson evokes different reactions from the strong Keith image. *Edinburgh City Libraries.*

CHAPTER 3

The early 1850's were important years for the progress of photography in Britain. 1853 had seen the establishment of the Photographic Society of London which would later develop into the Royal Photographic Society of today. The two dominant processes of the time, waxed paper and wet collodion, were the subject of considerable experiment throughout the country, and a healthy exchange of information was beginning to grow between photographers.

In the summer of 1855 Thomas Keith turned his camera towards the landmarks of his native city and produced an extensive series of Edinburgh monuments during the months of July, August, and September of that year. The series included naturally not only traditional views of well-known buildings but also a number of highly individual compositions. He was apparently working at least part of the time with John Forbes White, and the two men travelled extensively together throughout Scotland and the North of England. Their friendship, which had grown up in their Marischal days, and which developed through their joint love of photography – Keith the teacher and White the pupil – was cemented still more strongly when, some years later, White married Ina Johnston, Keith's sister-in-law.

Often the only difference between their pictures was in negative size – with White placing his camera in exactly the same spot as Keith, his teacher. Their relationship at this stage was clearly one of master and pupil with Keith the more technically accomplished of the two and by far the more creative. Work produced by White on his own has a primitive character which places it quite apart from Thomas Keith.

It appears however that this was not always the case. While in their early days working together there is a clear distinction of style, White later began to evolve and develop a style of his own. Much of the material in the various collections of Keith/White material has been classified purely on the basis of style or on an even more arbitrary basis; but quite often the tradition behind particular images has led to even greater confusion. During the research for this book a print, nominally by Keith, entitled 'on the Don' and in the Gernsheim Collection in Texas, was brought to my notice. This picture had been given to Gernsheim via Neven du Mont who had acquired it from Gertrude Keith, one of Thomas's daughters. She apparently gave du Mont the print as being one of her father's favourites. Later, in the archives of the Edinburgh Photographic Society, the negative came to light – initialled 'JFW' but not in White's handwriting. This picture had been passed down through White's family as one of *his* favourites. Certainly on neg-

ative size and physical characteristics it *is* by White, although, using previous accepted criteria, a judgement on the basis of its aesthetic value would attribute it to Keith. It must logically be by John Forbes White, but this of course immediately throws established ideas into confusion, and we must conclude that White was capable of work of a very much higher aesthetic order than had previously been admitted.

The interchange of ideas was extended in the following year when a group of Scottish photographers, including Keith and White, were instrumental in the formation of the Photographic Society of Scotland. The Society approached Thomas Sutton, editor and publisher of *Photographic Notes,* one of the livelier journals of the period, and Sutton agreed that the journal should act as the official organ of the new society. This led to the regular publication, for a time at least, of the group's proceedings, and these included several important contributions to photography by its members, who included Sir David Brewster, D. O. Hill, G. W. Wilson and others, as well as Keith and White.[1]

In one issue of the magazine Thomas Keith's important account of the waxed paper process was published in full and in another comments he had made on the problems of photography in Edinburgh:

'Dr Keith also shewed some negatives (on Rive's Paper), which had been injured by an excess of free iodine in the iodizing solution, the effect being visible in a number of small white spots in the negative; and in illustration of his remarks on the effect of smoke in the atmosphere, he exhibited two views from the same spot of the Castle of Edinburgh, of which one taken while there was a thick haze of smoke between the object and the camera, was, though pretty intense in the blacks, of a uniform grey or *muzzy* colour in the lights; the other, taken immediately after, when a breeze of wind just happened to clear away the smoke, was brilliant and vigorous.'[2]

Edinburgh, Auld Reekie, was no stranger to pollution even in those days!

In June of that same year – 1856 – Keith compiled his important paper for the Society on the waxed paper process and this was published in the July 17th edition of *Photographic Notes.* In his preface to the paper Thomas Sutton heralded the method as the simplest yet devised for the le Gray process – a claim which was not strictly true as Sutton was reminded by several readers in the issues of the Journal which followed. In fact in the *Photographic Journal,* the official organ of the London Photographic Society (now the RPS) another version of the process, using two chemicals fewer than Keith's method, had been published a few weeks earlier. There can be little doubt, however, that Thomas Keith's paper was a significant contribution to the published history of the process, for, as will be seen by reading the paper in Appendix 1, he brought to the process

12 The Royal Mile from Princes Street Gardens. *Private Collection.*

13 The Castle and West Princes Street Gardens. *Edinburgh City Libraries.*

These two pictures were one of the 'pairs' used in the early part of the research which led to this book and enabled the authorship of the private collection of negatives to be established.

Alvin Langdon Coburn, that early champion of Keith's photography, selected several of Keith's Greyfriars pictures from the albums he was shown by Thomas's daughters. He had platinum prints made from them and exhibited at the Royal Photographic Society Exhibition in 1914. It is interesting that Coburn selected three of the Greyfriars pictures for exhibition – their simple and direct approach being quite distant from

14 The Covenanter's Tomb, Greyfriars. *International Museum of Photography.*

15 The Covenanter's Tomb, Greyfriars. *Private Collection.*

the type of material Coburn was producing himself and which was also exhibited at the same time.

They do show clearly that, in skilled hands, the technical quality possible with the paper negative was not far short of that possible with collodion on glass.

The landscape picture is on remarkably thin paper – and may well be the thin 'Canson' paper of which Keith spoke in his lecture.

16 Bloody McKenzie's Tomb, Greyfriars. *International Museum of Photography.*

17 Bloody McKenzie's Tomb, Greyfriars. *Victoria and Albert Museum.*

These form part of an extensive series of lighting variations on this tomb which doubtless taught Dr Keith a great deal in his early experiments.

a much clearer understanding of the chemistry involved than had hitherto been available.

He was a modest man and, completely in character, claimed little for his expertise, starting his lecture to the Society with the words 'I have nothing original to offer you . . . .' Not only did he have a considerable expertise to offer in the field of photographic technology, but his creative contribution to the infant art was also immense – outweighing even his own technique. The true impact of his photography, although recognised by associates in his day, is only really clear with hindsight.

In the early years of practical photography one of the major problems encountered by photographers – both amateur and professional – was that of acceptance by the establishment. Was photography an art? Was it a simple scientific method of making an objective record?

Within the first few years of his calotype process Talbot had shown that photography could be much more than a mere recording medium by his use of varying lighting techniques on some of his early photographs of statues and busts. He had also come up against the traditional view of the painter with regard to vertical perspective. While a vanishing point had long been an accepted norm in painting (and is little more than horizontal convergence) vertical convergence – such as is always obtained when a camera is tilted upwards – was apparently too much for the art world to accept. This particular photographic phenomenon had been demonstrated in several of Talbot's early calotypes and in particular by *The Open Door*, one of the early illustrations in *The Pencil of Nature*, Talbot's showcase of photography.[3]

Talbot wrote to Herschel at one point expressing his views on the matter and suggesting, perhaps for the first time, that the accepted standards of painting should not necessarily be applied to photography. What he had in mind was clearly far from what actually happened. The criteria by which photographs were judged were certainly not the same as were used to judge paintings. All too often the technical and chemical considerations were given prominence over the aesthetic. It was, sadly, the rule rather than the exception for criticisms of photographs to be almost exclusively limited to a study of the success with which the process had been used, in many cases almost totally ignoring the pictures which had resulted. This had the effect of making many photographers less selective in content, and much more aware of technique – a 'photograph for its own sake' became an accepted justification of anything produced through the camera lens.

This state of affairs survived for a considerable number of years – in fact well after Thomas Keith's brief encounter with photography had come to an end. There is even a recorded account of some of Hill and Adamson's finest works being included in an exhibition in the 1880's as little more than examples of the 'primitive' calotype process, without reference to the vast contribution to the art of photography which these images represented.

In Keith's own day, the mood was even more banal. To

take a sheet of paper through a well documented series of steps and finish up with an image – any image – often earned a photographer considerable praise from the press. Only rarely in those early days would a review comment on the composition and tonal relationships within the image.

While Keith was clearly a master of technique, had he been nothing more than that we would not remember his photography today. Even if his work had taken the practical potential of photography to its limits, it would still have been overshadowed by his technical skill as a surgeon and physician. But his photography, especially in the later years of his short affair with the medium, was of the order of high art. To make this quite clear, it is essential to divorce the early Greyfriars experiments from the remainder of his work. He then emerges as a true artist, understanding a new medium, exploiting its possibilities to the full and endowing photography with the beginnings of a strong design heritage.

So often in the course of the researches for this book, I have come across references to Keith's work being 'as good as Hill's' or 'like Hill's'. One early account of Keith's work, wrongly attributing his photographs to the calotype process, appeared in *Calotypes by D O Hill and Robert Adamson selected from his collection by Andrew Elliot* written by John M. Gray in 1885 and published in 1928. Scottish photographers working in the early days of photography will no doubt always stand a little in the shadows of Hill and Adamson. A photographer who was also working with paper negatives had a particularly difficult task in achieving recognition. Keith's work was highly praised in his own lifetime – and the process he was using was clearly defined. It is the descending mist of time which has blurred the distinctions of process and blurred the obvious differences in style which marked Hill, Adamson, and Keith as individuals.

Keith's pictures are bold, striking and, above all else, personal statements. While other photographers, both amateur and professional, were still concerned with, and concentrating on, the photo-mechanical steps involved in producing a picture, Dr Keith was enlarging on his early art training by studying and coming to terms with the nature of light itself. While for other photographers light merely made their photography possible, for Thomas Keith light was often the very reason for photography. While others merely lit their compositions, to Keith the character of the light itself became a vital part of the composition, often inspiring it. While for others the subject was of prime importance, to Keith it was seldom more than a prop – one of the elements which contributed to his striking graphic compositions. His work is, at the same time, topographical and elemental. It conveys the atmosphere and the essence of the place without necessarily describing its physical attributes. In his approach he was clearly ahead of his time.

The reader could be forgiven for believing that there was little or no creative photography at this time. So much of the written account of photography's early years is based on

18 Group of Photographers at Craigmillar Castle, 1856. *Edinburgh City Libraries.*

19 Stereo pair from which (18) is enlarged. There is some confusion about the identification of the members of the Photographic Society of Scotland represented in this picture. Some sources believe that the gentleman sitting against the wall at the back with his hand to his face is Keith. But on close comparison with known portraits of Dr Keith, I believe that he is the gentleman leaning on the camera at the front of the group. Certainly the camera is of the size and type which Keith used. *Edinburgh City Libraries.*

contemporary publications and they, as we have said, considered the technical to the exclusion of the aesthetic. The survival of the creative reputations of several photographers appears to have relied heavily on their position in the art/photography world at the time. Thus Hill as Secretary of the Royal Scottish Academy was assured a reputation as more than a mere manipulator while Adamson, now revealed as an equal partner in the production of their most successful pictures, was given credit for little more than the

20 West End of Chambers Street. One of Keith's classic studies of the random shapes and textures which are the essence of the character of mediaeval Edinburgh. Compare this with the equally successful 'Back of the South Side of the Grassmarket' (plate 11). *Edinburgh City Libraries.*

22 Old Houses, Edinburgh. *International Museum of Photography.*

21 Brown Square, Chambers Street. A location which, in addition to its obvious photographic attractions, had medical links which might have drawn Thomas Keith to it. Here in 1824 James Syme, with whom Keith was currently working at Edinburgh Infirmary, had started the Brown Square Medical School. *Edinburgh City Libraries.*

chemistry. Roger Fenton, Julia Margaret Cameron and others were assured of their continued reputation, likewise because of position or associates. For Thomas Keith and many other amateurs whose greatest achievements lay in their professions, photographic reputations have been ignored over the years, while photography's history was written around the established figures.

By 1854-5 a clearly personal style had been evolved by Keith which amounted to a personal discovery of a new means of expression. The result is a superb series of pictures embodying an exploration of the hidden mysteries of Edinburgh. A strong relationship between the photographer and his subject can be seen through his views of the closes, the back streets, the vennels, and the buildings which formed the jumble left over from mediaeval Edinburgh. The view is new and revealing – emerging as an extensive study in line and texture, in shape and tone – a timeless approach to an already vanishing world.

He turned his camera towards subjects and conditions which he knew best suited the process he was using, and under his own rigorously enforced rules produced a new marriage of technical and artistic excellence. The same driving ambition which drove Hill and Adamson to the limits of the capabilities of their cameras and the calotype process, led Keith to equally ambitious but quite different heights. It was this recurrent theme of line and pattern with which he lifted amateur photography out of the role of

24 Iona Cathedral and nunnery ruins. *Iona Cathedral Trust.*

23 Iona Cathedral ruins. *Iona Cathedral Trust.*

25 Iona – nunnery ruins. These three images together with the series reproduced as plates 49-56 constitute the last dated series of pictures taken by Dr Keith. In the series as a whole, his understanding of the effective use of lighting, camera position, and elevation, his use of perspective and so on are all clearly evident. *Iona Cathedral Trust.*

26 Holyrood Abbey, West Doorway. The first of a long series of pictures of this delightful ruin. The cropping may at first seem peculiar, missing as it does the top of the ornate archway, but this may have been intentional, to draw attention to the dark interior through the doorway. However, as the print has been cropped extensively, such a decision was certainly not made at the time the picture was taken. It is interesting to note the architectural accuracy of the photograph. The camera has been kept absolutely level (essential if the shape of a building is to be maintained), thus bringing in a little foreground at the expense of detail at the top of the frame. *Scottish National Portrait Gallery.*

27 Multiple Exposure. No contemporary print exists of this surprising negative nor, perhaps even more surprising, do individual negatives of each constituent exposure. *Edinburgh City Libraries.*

28 Stereo photograph of unknown farmhouse. This interesting pair of waxed paper stereo negatives is assumed to be by Keith, as it was located with twelve other negatives apparently all by him. No contemporary prints exist of this exposure either. Perhaps neither technique appealed to Keith. *Private Collection.*

simple recorder. The skilful use of light emphasises and enhances; the careful use of weight and tone makes clear and decisive statements. Through many of his pictures Edinburgh could be seen as never before – the familiar now redefined.

It is relatively easy for us today, familiar with the potential of photography, to translate the mental image into a photographic image. In the mid-1850's, it was not quite as easy. As we have read, Talbot had come to terms with the totally different way of seeing with a lens – but that way of seeing would not have appealed to Thomas Keith. He too apparently felt that vertical convergence was a distortion and therefore went to considerable lengths to ensure that it

played no part in his picture-making. Not for him the simple task of tilting the camera at ground level to include the tops of buildings. In many cases he appears to have used tall tripods, or viewpoints halfway up nearby buildings to ensure that buildings were of recognisable shape. To him control was the essence of success. To many in the art world however he was offering clear proof that photography was not an art. Many painters claimed that, as photography was solely dependent on light, the photographer need only be an unskilled intermediary. (Photographers often retorted that painting was likewise dependent solely on pigments and brushes.) Many considered that, if photography was to be regarded as an art form, its role must be that of imitator, producing photographically what had hitherto been produced by the artist's brush. To Keith and others the dual role of photography – as recorder and as creative tool – seems to have been quite clear. The problems of equating and uniting the two posed a series of challenges to which he willingly rose.

Keith's understanding of lighting and his ability to control its effect is faultless, and reveals a sympathy with his subject which had not hitherto been demonstrated quite so effectively. Even Hill and Adamson had only rarely deviated from a particular quality of lighting – in a series of superb backlit views of St Andrews and Newhaven – and they had been much more immediately concerned with the juxtaposition of figures in their Calton Hill studio than with the quality of the light falling upon them. Lengthy series of pictures of the same tombs at Greyfriars had done for Keith's knowledge of lighting what photographs of busts had done for Talbot. Keith, however, had progressed very much further, using light as a means of creating atmosphere rather than merely of varying appearance. Bloody Mackenzie's tomb at Greyfriars appears under soft shadowless lighting, under weak sun, and under strong sun, teaching the photographer much about the quality of the medium with which he was working. Very early on in his short involvement with photography he had learned that lighting, used carelessly, can detract and confuse. Used skilfully, it can raise even an apparently mundane subject to the highest levels of beauty.

Working early or late in the day – his stated ideal – he presents us with a series of dramatic effects – long shadows reaching out from imposing shapes. Textures are clearly defined, architectural features isolated and exploited, always within carefully considered compositions, where the spacial and tonal relationships appear always to be totally controlled. As his photography was confined to what little spare time he had, his ideal conditions were initially enforced rather than created. It is however certain that he learned to understand fully and to exploit these conditions, turning practical necessity into aesthetic. What had been introduced for expediency became an integral part of his vision.

While many of his pictures are primarily descriptive, with others the location is quite incidental. Yet they unite to offer one of the most interesting visual accounts of Edinburgh in the last century. This analytical view of the city and the elements which are combined in it, is the essence of Keith's contribution to photography. Many of his pictures are simply geometric patterns. In one location, the doorway of Acheson House in the Canongate, he has encapsulated his ideas of photography's duality – as both recorder and vehicle for personal expression. In one of two views of a simple doorway, lit by oblique strong lighting, the stark outline of the doorway itself, opening into a total blackness beyond, is transformed into a piece of powerful design. The strong linear shape thus produced accentuates the hardness of the stone, the solidity of its structure. Above, the legend and date stand out strong and clear. A well perceived image acting as simple record. In the second version careful positioning of the shape of a woman, her shawls gently breaking the strong straight line of the stonework, turns that strong shape into a simple frame to draw the eye to, and accentuate, the softer contours of the figure herself. What was in the first the essence of the picture itself had become in the second merely an element within it.

This use of strong oblique lighting helped Keith to isolate his subject from its surroundings and thus accentuate it. The technique is used again at Iona in 1856 on several occasions. Keith and his wife holidayed at Iona in September and, during a brief stay, he combined the total achievement of his photography in a short but brilliant series of pictures. At St Oran's Chapel, that same oblique lighting turns the semi-circular Romanesque doorway into pure design – a diagonal shadow cutting through the opening to isolate the tooth-carving of the archway. Again, the 'Arches of the Chapter House at Iona' stand alone amidst blackness to concentrate and focus attention on their ornate stonework.

In a simple view of a lancet window, again at Iona, a second technique of isolation is employed; the small plain window, through which a strong black shadow-shape can be perceived, stands apparently alone in a sea of stonework. The sheer distance beween the edges of the image and the window itself, and the monotony of texture in between, is the strongest possible surround for this simple and powerful shape.

Very few of his contemporaries used lighting skilfully, settling for the conditions that prevailed, in preference to exercising the ultimate control and leaving the cameras in their cases. In this way – translating clear mental ideas into practical terms – he turned many subjects which his contemporaries might have overlooked into images they could not ignore.

Equally dependant on lighting – this time soft and subtle and more in keeping with his own 'ideal' – is an image entitled originally 'Iona, Sept. 1st' 56'. This image was later exhibited at the first exhibition of the Photographic Society of Scotland in December 1856 and described in *Photographic Notes* by Thomas Sutton as 'a vigorous and most powerful picture'. For the exhibition it was retitled 'Pillars of the Cathedral at Iona' and is for me the one picture which most easily sums up the genius of

29 The Castle from Johnston Terrace, August 17th 1855. *International Museum of Photography.*

Thomas Keith. The composition is superb – and the use of the figure of his wife to emphasise scale is perfect both in positioning and effect. The artistic merit of the picture depends on, and is enhanced by, its sheer technical excellence. No other lighting conditions would have produced such an evocative statement on the delightful ruined cathedral and, I believe, no other contemporary process could have conveyed that feeling so completely. Here is the master-photographer, working with a process and a subject entirely sympathetically.

It is this use of technique as a vital but unobtrusive ally to his own creative genius which stands Keith apart from others. To many technique came first – and all too often stood alone. To Thomas Keith technical perfection was a necessity, if his visual perception was to be translated into pictures.

Through the dark soft interior of the cathedral Keith looked out into the lighter, roofless, aisle with its sharply defined weed-covered stonework. The result is a romantic masterpiece which was rightly heralded in its own day as one of the finest pictures ever taken on paper. That it was taken by an amateur so early in the history of photography is one of the many surprises of Keith's work. This image and so many others produced by Thomas Keith deny their great age; they could have been produced yesterday.

While that particular picture stands brilliantly on its own, it has even more to say about the photographer when seen alongside 'Columns, Iona', produced the same day, and using as its subject the same pillars. Where the first view describes the cathedral aisle as tall, light, and airy, the second image, by careful selection of viewpoint, and this time with no clue as to scale, gives a powerful sense of weight and solidity.

In the series of photographs of Edinburgh we find that same ability to recognise and isolate the interesting feature, the contrast or the harmony. The themes of line and texture show up again in pictures of the rooftops of the Grassmarket where, in one image, the strong shapes and textures of crow-stepped gables, part in sun, part in shadow, form a strong thrusting 'V', drawing the viewer up to the solid mass of the castle rock and the buildings on top, while, in another, those same rooftops, chimneypots and variations in texture form a descriptive patchwork which captures perfectly the haphazard harmony of the old city.

In addition to this obvious consideration for the overall image, there is considerable evidence of Thomas Keith's almost obsessive attention to detail – with numerous slight variations of content in almost identical pictures. The Castle and the Grassmarket photographed from an elevated position – presumably one of the staircases leading up and out of the Grassmarket – was the subject for several different views. In three identical views only the positioning of carts and other odds and ends in front of the shops varied. Research has failed to reveal which, in the photographer's mind, was the most successful. It is clear however that some feature of the picture – whether it be technical or aesthetic – did not match up to his expectation and thus required a return.

POSTSCRIPT TO CHAPTER 3

One of Thomas Keith's earliest photographic expeditions – to Braemar in 1854, and his last – to Iona in September 1856, had been in the company of his wife Elizabeth. For the remainder of his short photographic career he worked either alone (on most of the Edinburgh pictures) or in the company of John Forbes White (at Roslin, St Andrews and elsewhere).

The number of their joint expeditions appears to have been considerable, and the men became very close friends. Their joint decision to abandon photography in 1857 must have made such a move easier for each man to bear. Keith devoted the remainder of his working life to medicine; White to running his Aberdeenshire mills and to his other great love – collecting antiques and paintings.

During the preceding five years Keith had been something of an innovator. As well as his personal variations on the waxed paper process, he had dabbled briefly with stereoscopy – and one pair of stereo negatives survives. Additionally, in 1856 he had produced what appears to be the earliest multiple exposure – an attempt, through six or seven exposures on a single sheet of paper, to produce the definitive photographic image of Edinburgh. There is just one example of this technique – and we must accept it was by design rather than accident, as Keith would not mistakenly expose the same sheet six times. We must therefore conclude that he did not really like what he had produced. Perhaps the idea arrived too late for him to develop it fully – there is no doubt that by early 1857 demands on his time were increasing. Whatever the reason, that single image remains, successfully in my opinion, as further proof of the modernity of Thomas Keith's vision.

Thomas Keith took time to set up his large camera and take a picture. With a 5/8th of an inch aperture in his large lens he would carefully remove the lens cap (there were no shutters in those days) and count off the seconds and minutes required to expose the negative.

The year after he retired from photography the world's first instantaneous picture – taken in Princes Street and showing for the first time the bustle of Scotland's capital – was taken by his friend from the Photographic Society of Scotland, George Washington Wilson of Aberdeen.

Wilson achieved his great landmark in photography not with the large camera and the paper negative, but with a small stereo camera and a specially modified version of the wet collodion process. That particular advance in the techniques and possibilities of photography quickly encouraged the demise of the waxed paper process. Thomas Sutton, writing in *Photographic Notes*, commented 'how infinitely superior to those "cities of the dead" with which we have hitherto been compelled to content ourselves'.

Perhaps Keith foresaw the changing mood of photography.

Keith, like Wilson, White, Hill and Adamson, Tunny, Walker and many others about whom research must continue, have given Scotland a rich and unique photographic heritage.

30 Mrs Keith and Ina Johnston (later Mrs John Forbes White). This picture, attributed to Dr Keith by his daughter, Gertrude, is his only known portrait. The two ladies were first cousins to the wife of James Young Simpson, Keith's friend and mentor. Thomas Keith and Elizabeth Johnston married in 1854; John Forbes White and Ina Johnston about three years later. *Gernsheim Collection, University of Texas.*

THE PLATES

Thomas Keith

It is not surprising that Scotland should have provided some of the finest early photographers in the light of the evangelical zeal with which the Scots adopted any new style idea or invention. Many of the pioneering experiments with Fox Talbot's calotype process – used by D. O. Hill, Robert Adamson and others – were carried out in Edinburgh and St Andrews. The field of optical science owes a great deal to another Scot, David Brewster, whose early exploits both as editor of the *Edinburgh Magazine* at the age of only twenty and in the field of advanced optical design, made him famous before Victoria came to the throne.

Edinburgh's tradition in art and science goes back a long way, and produced some fine paradoxes. The old city to which Thomas Keith arrived in 1845 was essentially mediaeval in character, clinging tightly round the castle rock, almost divorced from the clean elegance of the Georgian New Town to the north. Although Keith chose addresses in the New Town – Northumberland Street, North Char-

lotte Street and, later in life, Great Stuart Street, he found the mediaeval decay of the Old Town irresistable.

Edinburgh may have had its sights set clearly on the future, but its feet were still firmly rooted in its illustrious past; modern ideas set against a mediaeval backdrop. It is that contrast which is one of the strong attractions of the work of the early photographers.

The picturesque romance of the past and the pioneering spirit of discovery are neatly and superbly encapsulated in the series of Thomas Keith's photographs which follows.

Not only photographers will derive pleasure from them. They form a unique and personal account of mid-Victorian Scotland in terms of both its architecture and its atmosphere.

For the photographic historian, full details of the photographic aspects of each image are given where possible, followed by short topographical and historical notes on their locations.

VIEWS OF EDINBURGH

GREYFRIARS CHURCHYARD

The present church dates from 1612 when it was the first church to be established in Edinburgh after the Reformation. The site has been occupied by religious buildings since the 13th-century monastery of the Greyfriars was founded by a small community of Dutch friars. It was here that the famous National Covenant of 1638 was signed, traditionally laid out on a table tombstone, in which Scottish Protestants declared their total opposition to the establishment of the Anglican faith in Scotland by Charles I. Also in the churchyard is the roofless prison where many of the Covenanters were held prisoner in 1679. A memorial to them, known alternatively as the Covenanter's Memorial or the Martyr's Monument, was the subject of several of Thomas Keith's photographs (see figs 14 and 15 in the text).

In addition to the tombs portrayed in Thomas Keith's photographs, the churchyard also contains the grave of the Earl of Morton, the Regent of Scotland in the early reign of James VI, who was executed in 1581.

Plate 1
The Castle from Greyfriars Churchyard
Negative: Edinburgh City Libraries
Contemporary Print: Gernsheim Collection, University of Texas at Austin
Courtesy of Edinburgh City Libraries
276mm × 269mm

Plate 2
Detail of a Tomb, Greyfriars
Negative: International Museum of Photography, George Eastman House, New York
Contemporary Print: none known
Courtesy of the International Museum of Photography
277mm × 252mm

Plate 3
Foliage on a tombstone, Greyfriars (Tomb of John Byres of Coates)
Negative: Edinburgh City Libraries
Contemporary Print: private collection, Paris
Courtesy of Edinburgh City Libraries
251mm × 279mm

Plate 4
Tomb of Sir Hugh McCulloch, Greyfriars
Negative: International Museum of Photography
Contemporary Print: Royal Scottish Academy
Courtesy of the International Museum of Photography
245mm × 280mm

Plate 5
Tomb of John Naysmythe, Greyfriars
Negative: Edinburgh City Libraries
Contemporary Print: none known
Courtesy of Edinburgh City Libraries
225mm × 252mm

THE CASTLE

Edinburgh Castle dominates the city – both in actual terms and in reputation. The city grew up outside and surrounding the massive rock and the Castle itself dates in part from the late 11th century. It is certain however that a fortress has existed on this site for considerably longer. The Castle's dominance over the city sets the character of Edinburgh – and the early need for the Castle's protection set the style of architecture for centuries – closely grouped buildings, tall for their time to save building further from the fortress. Edinburgh tenements were tall before other cities in Scotland even dreamed of building upwards. The high buildings, linked by a maze of closes, vennels, and courtyards are the essential character of the city, captured so successfully in Thomas Keith's photographs. It is an interesting comment on the 'order' of the New Town, built to the north of Princes Street Gardens, that Keith's photography is exclusively concerned with the old hillside city.

From Princes Street Gardens looking south, few pictures of the Castle are possible which make it an integral part of the city. Looking north from the Grassmarket, from Johnston Terrace and Castle Terrace, and from Greyfriars itself, countless interesting views caught Thomas Keith's eye.

Plate 6
Castle from the Grassmarket
Negative: Edinburgh City Libraries
Contemporary Print: Gernsheim Collection
Courtesy of the Gernsheim Collection
253mm × 278mm

Plate 7
Castle from the Grassmarket
Negative: International Museum of Photography
Contemporary Print: none known
Courtesy of the International Museum of Photography
252mm × 279mm

Plate 8
Castle from the Grassmarket
Negative: Kodak Museum, Harrow (from a private collection)
Contemporary Print: Royal Scottish Academy
Courtesy of the Royal Scottish Academy
248mm × 279mm

Plate 9
Castle and the Magdalen Chapel from George IV Bridge
Negative: Edinburgh City Libraries
Contemporary Print: Gernsheim Collection
Courtesy of Edinburgh City Libraries
278mm × 243mm

Plate 10
Castle over the rooftops of the Grassmarket
Negative: Edinburgh City Libraries
Contemporary Print: Gernsheim Collection
Courtesy of Edinburgh City Libraries
258mm × 240mm

THE GRASSMARKET

The Grassmarket has seen some violent events in its long history. After firing on a crowd of citizens who refused to disperse in 1736, Captain Porteus was tried and eventually condemned to death for murder. After a reprieve he was dragged from the Tolbooth and hanged by the mob from a dyer's pole by the Grassmarket. The Grassmarket saw a considerable number of public executions – but perhaps none as emotive as the execution of some of the Covenanters whose memorial Thomas Keith photographed in Greyfriars. The religious feelings aroused by the trial of the Covenanters were fanned even higher by the judges sending the condemned men to 'praise God in the Grassmarket' – with all that the term implied .

The Grassmarket was originally the City's marketplace, where the farmers and the people from the surrounding countryside sold their wares.

The Cowgate, another source of several of Keith's pictures, leads into it.

The Lawnmarket, on the Royal Mile between the High Street and Castle Hill was the traditional merchant's market.

In Plate 12, the posters on the walls of the Grassmarket are particularly interesting – advertising a military spectacular based on the Battle of Alma. The battle was fought in September 1854 and this production at Edinburgh's Theatre Royal was staged in the following year.

Plate 11
Back of the south side of the Grassmarket
Negative: Edinburgh City Libraries
Contemporary Print: none known
Courtesy of Edinburgh City Libraries
253mm × 240mm

Plate 12
The Grassmarket
Negative: not known
Contemporary Print: Royal Scottish Academy
Courtesy of the Royal Scottish Academy
272mm × 240mm

Plate 13
Cardinal Beaton's House, Cowgate
Negative: International Museum of Photography
Contemporary Print: Royal Scottish Academy
Courtesy of the Royal Scottish Academy
241mm × 270mm

THE ROYAL MILE

Although Princes Street may be the best known of Edinburgh's streets, there is no doubt that for the tourist the Royal Mile is like a magnet. That steep hill between the Castle and the Palace of Holyroodhouse plays host to millions of visitors each year. In Thomas Keith's day Edinburgh life was a little less hectic, but the attraction of that famous mile was certainly just as great for the photographer as it is today.

'The Royal Mile' is in reality four streets – Castlehill, the Lawnmarket, the High Street, and Canongate, leading from the Castle Esplanade at the top to Abbey Strand and the Abbey and Palace at the bottom of the hill. This was the main thoroughfare of mediaeval Edinburgh, and was flanked by the houses of the rich merchants. The closes which run off the main steet lead into courtyards, ancient inns, narrow vennels, and steep stairways leading down to Cowgate to the south, Jeffrey Street, and Market Street to the north.

Much of the building work along the north side of th Royal Mile is late 16th century, with the south side, except for St Giles Cathedral, being on the whole a little later.

From the top of the hill, Keith progressed south photographing most of the interesting buildings at one time or another. His subjects included The Castle of course, Castle Hill, the Lawnmarket and West Bow (Bowhead House – so typical of mediaeval Edinburgh architecture), John Knox's House, the Canongate Tolbooth, Huntly House and Bakehouse Close, White Horse Close, Acheson House, and Holyrood Palace and Abbey.

John Knox's House, of 15th century origin, is traditionally the home of the leader of the Scottish Reformation although there is some doubt if he ever lived there. Like so many other houses in Scotland, it is also said to have been the one-time residence of Mary Queen of Scots, having been given to her by her goldsmith.

Canongate was originally a separate burgh within the City, and was therefore entitled to its own Tolbooth – Town House. The Canongate Tolbooth, a tall and elegant building was built in 1591 and is now, like John Knox's House, a museum. Huntly House and Bakehouse Close are slightly earlier, having been completed in 1517. Huntly House too is now a museum. White Horse Close, now carefully restored as a number of flats, was originally, in the 17th century, a coaching inn.

The foot of the 'Mile' is dominated by the Palace of Holyroodhouse and the adjoining ruins of the Augustinian Holyrood Abbey. The Abbey, founded in 1128, traditionally by King David I in thanksgiving for a safe deliverance from an attack by a stag in the woods outside the city. At the time of the Reformation, the monastic buildings were allowed to decay, while the church continued to be used until the roof collapsed in 1768. Today it remains much as it did in Thomas Keith's day. The Palace was founded in 1501 by James IV of Scotland and extended by James V. However during the 'Commonwealth' it was destroyed by fire while Cromwell's troops were billeted in it and much of the present building dates from a reconstruction by Sir William Bruce in the 17th century.

Plate 14
North Side of the Lawnmarket
Negative: Edinburgh City Libraries
Contemporary Print: Edinburgh City Libraries
Courtesy of Edinburgh City Libraries
248mm × 231mm

Plate 15
Bowhead House
Negative: Edinburgh City Libraries
Contemporary Print: none known
Courtesy of Edinburgh City Libraries
247mm × 250mm

Plate 16
Bowhead House
Negative: not known
Contemporary Print: Royal Scottish Academy
Courtesy of the Royal Scottish Academy
240mm × 275mm

Plate 17
John Knox House, High Street
Negative: Gernsheim Collection
Contemporary Print: none known
Courtesy of the Gernsheim Collection
275mm × 245mm

Plate 18
Canongate Tolbooth
Negative: Gernsheim Collection
Contemporary Print: Royal Scottish Academy
Courtesy of the Gernsheim Collection
248mm × 278mm

Plate 19
Bakehouse Close, Huntly House
Negative: International Museum of Photography
Contemporary Print: none known
Courtesy of the International Museum of Photography
221mm × 272mm

Plate 20
Doorway, Acheson House, Canongate
Negative: International Museum of Photography
Contemporary Print: none known
214mm × 257mm

Plate 21
Doorway, Acheson House, Canongate
Negative: Edinburgh City Libraries
Contemporary Print: Royal Scottish Academy
Courtesy of Edinburgh City Libraries
212mm × 256mm

Plate 22
White Horse Close, Canongate
Negative: not known
Contemporary Print: Royal Scottish Academy
Courtesy of the Royal Scottish Academy
242mm × 271mm

Plate 23
White Horse Close
Negative: Edinburgh City Libraries
Contemporary Prints: Royal Scottish Academy, Edinburgh City Libraries
Courtesy of the Royal Scottish Academy
270mm × 246mm

Plate 24
West doorway, Holyrood Abbey
Negative: Edinburgh City Libraries
Contemporary Print: Scottish National Portrait Gallery
Courtesy of the Scottish National Portrait Gallery
229mm × 249mm

Plate 25
Arcading, Holyrood Abbey
Negative: not known
Contemporary Print: Gernsheim Collection
Courtesy of the Gernsheim Collection
266mm × 234mm

Plate 26
East window, Holyrood Abbey
Negative: Edinburgh City Libraries
Contemporary Print: Royal Scottish Academy
Courtesy of the Royal Scottish Academy
242mm × 257mm

ELSEWHERE IN EDINBURGH

Plate 27
High School Wynd
Negative: Edinburgh City Libraries
Contemporary Prints: Royal Scottish Academy, Edinburgh City Libraries
Courtesy of the Royal Scottish Academy
246mm × 270mm

Plate 28
Unidentified close
Negative: not known
Contemporary Print: Royal Scottish Academy
Courtesy of the Royal Scottish Academy
245mm × 274mm

Plate 29
Doorway of Tailors Hall, Potterrow, East Portsburgh
Negative: Edinburgh City Libraries
Contemporary Print: none known
Courtesy of Edinburgh City Libraries
240mm × 252mm

Plate 30
Edinburgh – Multiple exposure
Negative: Edinburgh City Libraries
Contemporary Print: none known
Courtesy of Edinburgh City Libraries
276mm × 223mm

DISCOVERING THE COUNTRYSIDE

Thomas Keith travelled extensively in Scotland and turned his camera towards the simple compositions of nature as well as the architecture of the countryside. Quite a number of his pictures show that his self-made rules of working only in the middle of summer were sometimes ignored. The success of these pictures is such however that we can forgive him such slight deviations from his published principles. In Keith's day Blackford Farm was some miles from Edinburgh; now it is surrounded by the spread of Scotland's capital. The 'Pool at Blackford Farm' and the superb 'Avenue of Trees at Drum' remain his finest landscapes. Sadly the locations of many of these pictures are unknown.

Plate 31
Blackford Farm, May 10th 1856
Negative: Edinburgh City Libraries
Contemporary Print: Gernsheim Collection
Courtesy of the Gernsheim Collection
271mm × 241mm

Plate 32
Logs and gable, Blackford Farm, May 10th 1856
Negative: Edinburgh City Libraries
Contemporary Print: Gernsheim Collection
Courtesy of Edinburgh City Libraries
192mm × 210mm

Plate 33
Pool, Blackford Farm, May 10th 1856
Negative: Gernsheim Collection
Contemporary Print: Gernsheim Collection
Courtesy of the Gernsheim Collection
261mm × 223mm

Plate 34
Avenue of trees at Drum
Negative: private collection
Contemporary Print: none known
Reproduced by kind permission of the owner
274mm × 212mm

Plate 35
Fallen trees, Braemar, June 1854
Negative: Edinburgh City Libraries
Contemporary Print: Gernsheim Collection
Courtesy of Edinburgh City Libraries
252mm × 212mm·

Plate 36
Treescape 1
Negative: Edinburgh City Libraries
Contemporary Print: none known
Courtesy of Edinburgh City Libraries
244mm × 213mm

Plate 37
Treescape 2
Negative: Edinburgh City Libraries
Contemporary Print: none known
Courtesy of Edinburgh City Libraries
204mm × 251mm

Plate 38
Treescape 3
Negative: Edinburgh City Libraries
Contemporary Print: none known
Courtesy of Edinburgh City Libraries
254mm × 206mm

Plate 39
Unidentified boats
Negative: Edinburgh City Libraries
Contemporary Print: none known
Courtesy of Edinburgh City Libraries
226mm × 262mm

AROUND SCOTLAND

A favourite haunt of Thomas Keith's was the town of Inverkeithing, across the River Forth from Edinburgh. Inverkeithing has some fine old buildings and several of Keith's pictures here strongly echo Hill and Adamson's pictures at St Andrews. Gala House, Fordell's House, Anderson House, the Tolbooth, and the Mercat Cross all feature in an extensive series of pictures produced c.1856. The plates in this section also include a fine study of Dryburgh Abbey, the West Port at St Andrews, and a delightful study of the small port of Dysart.

The Royal Burgh of Linlithgow boasts one of the finest mediaeval fortress/palaces in Britain and was for a time the home of the Kings of Scotland. Nearby a port, heavily fortified, was built at Blackness. The Church of St Michael was founded 1242 and predates the adjoining palace by almost 200 years.

Plate 40
St Michael's Church, Linlithgow
Negative: private collection
Contemporary Print: none known
Reproduced by kind permission of the owner
273mm × 226mm

Plate 41
Courtyard, Linlithgow Palace
Negative: Edinburgh City Libraries
Contemporary Print: private collection, Paris
Courtesy of Edinburgh City Libraries
269mm × 267mm

Plate 42
Cloisters, Dryburgh Abbey
Negative: private collection
Contemporary Print: none known
Reproduced by kind permission of the owner
271mm × 220mm

Plate 43
Dysart
Negative: Edinburgh City Libraries
Contemporary Print: none known
Courtesy of Edinburgh City Libraries
245mm × 248mm

Plate 44
Doorway, Roslin Chapel
Negative: International Museum of Photography
Contemporary Print: Edinburgh City Libraries
Courtesy of the International Museum of Photography
248mm × 274mm

Plate 45
West Port, St Andrews
Negative: Edinburgh City Libraries
Contemporary Print: Edinburgh City Libraries
Courtesy of Edinburgh City Libraries
254mm × 230mm

Plate 46
Inverkeithing, Gala House
Negative: Edinburgh City Libraries
Contemporary Print: none known
Courtesy of Edinburgh City Libraries
254mm × 246mm

Plate 47
Old Houses, Inverkeithing
Negative: Edinburgh City Libraries
Contemporary Print: none known
Courtesy of Edinburgh City Libraries
233mm × 253mm

THOMAS KEITH AT IONA
SEPTEMBER 1856

From a photographic point of view, the series from which these eight prints are drawn is arguably Keith's finest. There is total sympathy with both subject and medium, combining to produce a totally descriptive, yet heavily evocative study of one of Scotland's most important and best-loved religious sites.

On this tiny island, St Columba established one of Scotland's first religious houses when he arrived from Ireland in 563 AD. From Iona, the spread of Christianity through Scotland was rapid and the island has been the site of a cathedral for centuries. The present cathedral dates predominantly from the late 15th/early 16th centuries but had, by Keith's day, been in ruins for a considerable period. St Oran's Chapel dates from 1080 and is said to have been founded by Scotland's saintly Queen Margaret. The nunnery, founded in 1203, is nearby.

The Cathedral was restored early this century and is now a popular place of pilgrimage again. The negatives from which the bulk of these plates are produced are now part of the Cathedral's treasures, administered by a charitable trust, the Iona Cathedral Trust.

Plate 48
Iona from the beach
Negative: Iona Cathedral Trust
Contemporary Print: none known
Courtesy of the Iona Cathedral Trust
278mm × 225mm

'If you were to ask me to what circumstance more than any other I attribute my success, I should say, not to any peculiarity whatever in my manipulation, or to any particular strength of solutions I employ, but entirely to this, that I never expose my paper, unless the light is first-rate. This I have now made a rule, and nothing ever induces me to deviate from it; and I may safely say that since I attended to this I have never had a failure.'

Thomas Keith
in a lecture to a meeting of the Photographic Society of Scotland June 1856.

Plate 1.   The Castle from Greyfriars Churchyard

Plate 2.   Detail of a Tomb, Greyfriars

Plate 3. Foliage on a tombstone, Greyfriars (Tomb of John Byres of Coates)

Plate 4.   Tomb of Sir Hugh McCulloch, Greyfriars

Plate 5.   Tomb of John Naysmythe, Greyfriars

30

Plate 6. Castle from the Grassmarket

Plate 7. Castle from the Grassmarket

Plate 8.   Castle from the Grassmarket

Plate 9.   Castle and the Magdalen Chapel from George IV Bridge

Plate 10. Castle over the rooftops of the Grassmarket

Plate 11. Back of the south side of the Grassmarket

Plate 12. The Grassmarket

Plate 13. Cardinal Beaton's House, Cowgate

Plate 14. North Side of the Lawnmarket

Plate 15. Bowhead House

Plate 16. Bowhead House

Plate 17. John Knox House, High Street

Plate 18. Canongate Tolbooth

Plate 19. Bakehouse Close, Huntly House

Plate 20. Doorway, Acheson House, Canongate

Plate 21. Doorway, Acheson House, Canongate

Plate 22. Whitehorse Close, Canongate

Plate 23. Whitehorse Close

Plate 24. West doorway, Holyrood Abbey

Plate 25. Arcading, Holyrood Abbey

Plate 26. East window, Holyrood Abbey

Plate 27. High School Wynd

52

Plate 28. Unidentified close

Plate 29. Doorway of Tailors Hall, Potterrow, East Portsburgh

Plate 30. Edinburgh – Multiple exposure

Plate 31. Blackford Farm, May 10th 1856

Plate 32. Logs and gable. Blackford Farm. May 10th 1856

Plate 33. Pool, Blackford Farm, May 10th 1856

Plate 34. Avenue of trees at Drum

Plate 35. Fallen trees, Braemar, June 1854

60

Plate 36. Treescape

Plate 37. Treescape

Plate 38. Treescape

Plate 39. Unidentified boats

Plate 40. St Michael's Church, Linlithgow

Plate 41. Courtyard, Linlithgow Palace

Plate 42. Cloisters, Dryburgh Abbey

Plate 43. Dysart

Plate 44. Doorway, Roslin Chapel

Plate 45. West Port, St Andrews

Plate 46. Inverkeithing. Gala House

Plate 47. Old Houses, Inverkeithing

Plate 48. Iona from the beach

Plate 49. Iona, the Cathedral ruins

Plate 50. Iona Cathedral, the Aisle

Plate 51. Iona, arches over Chapter House doorway

Plate 52. Iona, East Chapter House window

Plate 53. Doorway, St Oran's Chapel, Iona

Plate 54. Pillars of the Cathedral, Iona

Plate 55. Columns of the Cathedral, Iona

APPENDIX I

It is not often that we get the chance to read and study a complete account of a particular photographer's technique. It is the completeness of the following document which makes it of particular historic significance. The technique itself is not fundamentally different from many other users of the wax paper process but the apparent clarity of understanding of the total requirement of a photographic process places Keith's approach high above many of his contemporaries.

from *Photographic Notes* No. 8. July 17th, 1856

> The monthly meeting of the [Photographic] Society [of Scotland] was held on Tuesday, 10th June (1856) Mr. Moir, one of the Vice-Presidents, in the Chair.
> Dr. Thos. Keith read a paper on the Waxed paper process, (see below), and exhibited a number of his negatives. These were greatly admired, and were considered by the Secretary to be the finest that had yet been produced. The dark parts had great intensity, and the whites were perfectly transparent and pure; the middle tints were also well brought out, and showed all the detail with the smoothness and sharpness of glass negatives.[1] It will be seen that the modification of the waxed paper process which Dr. Keith recommended, and by which those negatives were produced, is much more simple in the composition of the iodizing solution than that usually employed. And in addition to Dr. Keith's own experience of the uselessness, or indeed injurious effect, of many of the substances generally added to that solution, such as cyanide and fluoride of potass, arsenic, alcohol, grape sugar, &c., some of the members who formerly employed the complex iodizing formula containing these, but who have now adopted the simple ingredients and proportions recommended by Dr. Keith, have found that by the latter preparation they produce pictures at least as good as by the former, with much greater certainty. Dr. Keith also showed some negatives (on *Rive's* paper), which had been injured by an excess of free iodine in the iodizing solution, the effect being visible in a number of small white spots on the negative; and in illustration of his remarks on the effect of smoke in the atmosphere, he exhibited two views from the same spot of the Castle of Edinburgh, of which one taken while there was a thick haze of smoke between the object and the camera, was, though pretty intense in the blacks, of a uniform grey or *muzzy* colour in the lights; the other, taken immediately after, when a breeze of wind happened to clear away the smoke, was brilliant and vigorous.'

Dr. Keith's Paper on the Waxed paper process

'I have nothing original to offer with regard to the process which I am about to lay before you this evening. The manipulation is in almost every respect identical to that of Le Gray; and though, in common with many others, I have found it convenient to change some of the proportions of some of the solutions as originally employed by him, still the process is essentially his – and I have merely this evening to describe a certain modification of his process, which seems to me more satisfactory in its results, and better adapted to our atmosphere. I shall also endeavour to show what an experience of two summers has taught me of the various causes of failure, and of the ways of preventing them.

I began with Le Gray's weak solutions, but soon found it impossible to get anything like a decent negative with them under an exposure of 30 or 40 minutes. The process in its original state was evidently not suitable for our climate, and the great waste of time rendered it a very unsatisfactory one for the amateur. Experience soon taught me however, that by increasing or decreasing the strength of the iodizing solution (and consequently by increasing or decreasing the amount of iodide of silver in the paper), almost any degree of sensitiveness could be procured, from the rapidity of collodion to the slowness of albumen.[2] I was thus enabled to get equally powerful negatives in one minute as in half an hour, the only difference in preparation of these being, that in the former the iodizing solution was about double the strength of that employed in the latter. I accordingly selected for the ordinary purposes of views of buildings and landscapes, such proportions as would require an exposure from three to five or six minutes. Such a paper allows a considerable latitude of exposure without the risk of solarization. A more sensitive paper than this I found could not be depended on, unless used within a very short time after preparation.

The process as thus modified, I believe to be a good one, and if you wax your own paper, it is not an expensive one. It is also economical as far as time is concerned, for everything connected with it is best done at night, when the work of the day is over.

To begin then with the paper. The best paper I ever had was some of Canson's thin negative, which I got from Sandford about three years ago. I have not been able since then to procure any of a similar quality. Turner's and Whatman's papers give excellent results, but the washing of English papers is very difficult, and therefore the thin French paper is preferable. What I now use has the mark "Rive" on some of the sheets. It does not give such fine detail as some of the other papers, but it is easily to be had, seems very uniform, and as far as I have found it, very free from spots. It has one peculiarity, however, which annoyed me for a long time. It is very freely sized with starch, and little particles of starch are scattered through it, so that if much free iodine be used in the iodizing solution, so as to give the paper a dark blue colour, a deposit of iodide of starch takes place in the paper, and the iodized paper when dry is seen to be covered with a multitude of black spots. These appear in the negative as innumerable white spots, and render it quite useless for printing. I have never met with this peculiarity in any other paper which I have tried. The remedy for it is either to use no free iodine in iodizing, or to use it in very minute quantity; or else, if much has been added, to keep the paper for a considerably longer time in the aceto-nitrate bath, till all these particles have been sufficiently acted upon.

With a little method the waxing of the paper is very simple, and by no means a laborious business. Latterly I have always waxed my own paper, as what I bought waxed was so bad that the half of it was generally useless. By doing it yourself you have it much better done, and it is much more economical than buying it waxed.

You proceed as follows:

Cut the papers the proper size, and dry each piece well before the fire; dry also the blotting paper, which should be thick, soft, and as absorbent as possible. You then take a piece of smooth iron plate (an oven shelf answers remarkably well), and place it in front of a strong fire. When sufficiently heated, which is when water dropped upon it boils without running off, put it on a board on a table, or in any other position, provided it be not a constrained one; place upon it a sheet or two of old blotting paper, or more if you think the plate has been too much heated; on this lay one of the papers to be waxed; rub a piece of wax rapidly over it, it becomes at once transparent; then add another and another sheet, rubbing each piece for an instant, till you have a thick mass of 30 or 40 pieces waxed. By this time the plate has cooled somewhat, and the wax is not so readily imbibed; you then, with half a cake of wax, press out as much as possible; collect the spare wax in a saucer, or some other convenient vessel, and lift up the sheets one by one, and let them cool. The plate is again to be heated as before. You may then repeat this part of the operation with as many more pieces, or proceed to iron those already waxed. Take 20 or more pieces of thoroughly dry blotting paper; place between each a sheet of waxed paper, lay the whole heap upon the heated plate, and, having placed a sheet or two of blotting paper to prevent the lower sheets from getting scorched, with a well heated iron begin ironing at the top of the mass, and you will find to your delight, that by the time you are satisfied with the appearance of the first two or three sheets, the whole number are uniformly transparent, the heat from the

I would recommend every one to iodize the paper for himself whether he wax it or not. There is no satisfaction in not knowing what you are working with. I think the iodized paper deteriorates by too long keeping, though a month or two does not seem to affect it. But I cannot speak positively on this subject. It should be kept in a portfolio, and handled as little as possible.

The next part of the process, the formation of the sensitive surface, is a very important one, and requires to be carefully managed. I am in the habit of using the ordinary strength of solutions, 30 grams of nitrate of silver to one oz of water and about 35 drops of glacial acetic acid. I use a large quantity of aceto-nitrate, not less than 12 or 15 oz in the same dish. I generally prepare half a dozen sheets at the same time, using two dishes and sensitizing a sheet in each; a great saving of time is thus obtained. It is necessary, however, to be very careful in keeping the papers moving about, to prevent them touching the bottom of the dish, or resting against each other, in order that the decomposition may be as complete and equal as possible. They must remain in the silver bath at least 10 or 12 minutes. They are then removed one by one, and washed in a large dish of plain water, blotted off, and placed in the slides.

A great secret in success is keeping the silver bath in good order. Every sheet immersed in it removes much silver, and there is a constant weakening of the bath going on. It is necessary, therefore, to keep making up this waste by adding silver to it from time to time. Using so strongly iodized paper as the above, the bath soon gets exhausted; and unless you leave your papers a much longer time in it than 10 minutes, or else keep adding fresh silver and acetic acid, you very soon find your negatives covered with white spots and patches, arising from the decomposition not having thoroughly taken place; or else they come up feeble and flat, just as they do with a weak bath in the collodion process. I have no rule for adding nitrate, but on average I should say I add one dram for every six sheets, and as much acetic acid. One must not be economical with the silver bath. The less so as it is so easy to recover it from the waste washing.[3]

The most absolute cleanliness is essential in this part of the process, and no straggling rays of white light should on any account be permitted to enter the dark room.

As to the keeping qualities of the paper, I cannot speak with any plate at the bottom has been transmitted through the whole and the superabundant wax absorbed, and you have nothing to do but remove the papers and insert others. The blotting paper will answer for a great many times. You may thus easily, without fatigue, prepare in two or three hours as much paper as the most active photographer would use in the course of a summer, and at about one sixth of the usual price, and what is more, much better ironed. The first time I tried waxing in the way usually done, it took me near half a night, with a number of irons, before I got one piece that pleased me.

The next step is the iodizing. I prefer the following solution. It is considerably stronger than that generally used.

To 40 oz of water add –

    750 grains of iodide of potassium
    250 grains of bromide of potassium
    3 oz Sugar of milk
    30 or 40 grains of common salt;

Add a grain or two of free iodine in order to give the paper a brown tinge; this latter greatly facilitates the detection of air bubbles in the next part of the process, but further than that, I think it is of no use.

Into this solution the papers are plunged one by one, removing air bubbles, and allowed to remain in it all night, when they are hung up to dry. It is better to prepare not more than 10 or 12 sheets in the same dish; if more are used at once, the iodizing is not so likely to be equally accomplished.

I have used gelatine, rice water, and other preparations recommended by many, but I do not believe they are of the slightest use; nor do I ever employ any of the salts of potass beyond the iodide and bromide, for the simpler the solutions are the better. In this part of the process one can hardly make any mistake.

degree of certainty. As far as my experience goes, however, I should say that it is uncertain, and not much to be depended upon. Certainly for

town work I prefer using it within 24 hours after it has been made sensitive. If you wish to keep it longer than that time, it ought to be kept in the slides, and not in the blotting paper. The presence of air seems to have a great effect in deteriorating its keeping qualities.[4] Last summer, for instance, I had prepared half a dozen pieces of paper, but on account of very wet weather had no opportunity of using them for 6 days afterwards. Three of them had been put into the slides immediately after being blotted off. These when developed turned out excellent negatives, the other three which had been kept in a portfolio, blackened immediately on being put into the gallic acid. Of course I do not mean to say that a paper prepared with weaker solutions than those I employ will not keep much longer; but I find that the fresher the paper, the better the negative.

My usual time of exposure with a single achromatic lens of 17 inch focus and 5/8 aperture, varies according to circumstances from 2 to 8 minutes. Last summer the average exposure with this method was about 4 minutes, in bright sunshine. The proper amount of exposure is, I am quite satisfied, the *sine qua non* in this process, as I believe, in every other. With freshly made paper, there is a considerable latitude allowable, but if the paper has been kept for some days, in my hands it has solarized very easily.

If you were to ask me to what circumstance more than any other I attribute my success, I should say, not to any peculiarity whatever in my manipulation, or to any particular strength of the solutions I employ, but entirely to this, that I never expose my paper, unless the light is first-rate. This I have now made a rule, and nothing ever induces me to deviate from it; and I may safely say that since I attended to this I have never had a failure. You are thus saved all the annoyance and vexation and loss of time in developing pictures which you know can never turn out satisfactory. Consequently I limit the time for taking negatives to a few weeks in the middle of summer. I sensitize my paper overnight, for in the middle of summer I am almost sure of clear mornings soon after sunrise, and most of my negatives have been taken before 7 in the morning, or after 4 in the afternoon.[5] The light then is much softer, the shadows are larger and the half tints in your picture are more perfect, and the lights more agreeable. If working during the height of the day, I prefer having partly diffused light, partly sunshine.[6]

If the exposure has been well timed, the development will I believe take care of itself.[7] You immerse the sheets in a freshly made saturated solution of gallic acid, and after they have remained a few minutes, and all the air bells are removed, you add your aceto-nitrate solution. If you are in a hurry and wish the picture developed quickly, that is in three quarters of an hour, which is my average, you add about one dram of aceto-nitrate to every 4 ounces of gallic acid solution. Any old aceto-nitrate answers quite well for this purpose. If you have not time to watch their development, add a few drops, 8 or 10, of glacial acetic acid to the gallic acid, and after immersion in this for a few minutes, add 5 or 6 drops of aceto nitrate. They will thus go on developing quite cleanly for some hours, and at your convenience you may rapidly finish the development by adding more of the silver solution. When the pictures are brought out to your mind, they are to be washed and fixed in the usual way.

So much for the routine of the process. Now as to the causes of failure. It is sometimes not easy to tell exactly to what one circumstance, or to what combination of circumstances, we are to attribute our failures. One man for instance says that one half the failures arise from using impure wax, another that more than one half arises from impure and weak acetic acid, while a third believes that dirt in the dishes has a good deal to do with them, and another blames the paper.

I am quite satisfied that the commonest cause of failure arises from the paper being exposed in bad or indifferent light, especially in town, where the atmosphere is so much adulterated with smoke. I never got a good picture when there was the slightest trace of that blue haze which smoke produces between the camera and the object. If you examine the air when smoke is present, with a lens, you will see it all in a state of vibration, and as it were composed of an innumerable number of small particles. The same effect is visible in the sultry weather of summer, or in the spring after the continuance of dry east winds. This is seen best, in a very exaggerated condition, in the Sirocco wind. This state of the atmosphere is most ruinous, even in the slightest degree, to the action of the actinic rays.

Another common cause of failure in this process arises, I believe, from our trusting too much in the keeping qualities of the paper. At all events I can say this at least, that since I made it a rule never to expose my paper unless in a clear bright light, and gave up using my paper beyond 24 hours after sensitizing, I think I may safely say that I never had a failure.

I cannot attribute any of my early failures to impure wax. What I use is the common yellow Hamburgh wax of the shops. I have also used it much adulterated with spermaceti, but I cannot say I experienced any difference.

I have the same to say with regard to weak or impure acetic acid. I have never met with failure arising from this cause; at least in nine tenths of my negatives I have used the common commercial acid, which however goes by the name of "glacial". This summer I have used the *real* glacial which crystallises at 50°F. But I cannot say that my negatives are the least degree better or clearer than those of last year. The only difference I can perceive is that one cost 4d and the other somewhere about 1 shilling per oz. If the acetic acid is weak, one must just add more of it, until one gets clean pictures.

What I have heard most of my friends who have tried this process complain of, is, the staining and marbling of the negative during development. Now this is a very easily rectified mistake. Those stains are caused by the paper being allowed to touch the bottom of the dish during the sensitizing part of the process, even if the dish be chemically clean; though they do not appear till the developing. They are easily remedied by using a large quantity of silver solution, and by keeping the dish moving, occasionally turning the sheets over. Of this I can speak with certainty.

Want of clearness of the lights of the negative arises, either from bad light during the exposure, or (if the light has been good), either from imperfect washing, or a want of acetic acid, either in the bath or in the silver afterwards added. It is easily remedied by adding acetic acid, which has a wonderful property of keeping everything clean.

Failures from under-exposure speak for themselves; those arising from over-exposure are very curious, and at first sight very puzzling. Pictures overexposed generally come up rapidly in the gallic acid, and appear to be all right, till on examining them by transmitted light, they are seen to have a reddish grey appearance all over, and the high lights are not deeper than the half tints.[8]

I need not add that dirt and uncleanliness in all stages are pretty sure to end in failures; and I am quite sure that a weak aceto-nitrate bath is often the cause of feeble negatives.

Such are my experiences and some of the commonest causes of failure.

I would recommend to any one who thinks of trying this method to keep his nitrate bath of good strength, never to expose in bad light, and to use the paper freshly sensitized, and I believe after a little practise he will find it will require some trouble to occasion a failure.'

Footnotes to Appendix I

[1] The idea that collodion automatically gave sharper, finer detailed images than any previously obtainable process is a myth which has grown up in the last fifty years of writing the history of photography. As I have previously mentioned, the major advantage of collodion was in ease of printing. There was the additional, specialist, requirement of dimensional stability, but this certainly did not concern the vast majority of photographers either amateur or professional.

[2] Albumen-on-glass was invented in the early 1840s by Abel Niepce de Saint Victor, the nephew of Joseph Nicéphore Niepce who, with Daguerre had set the foundations of photography in the 1820s and 1830s. This, and not wet collodion was the earliest practical process on glass but, like collodion when dry, the albumen-based emulsion was very insensitive. The process never achieved notable success outside France.

[3] We tend to think of silver recovery as being an idea born of our modern interest in ecology and conservation of limited resources. Keith, no doubt, was interested in the idea as a 'canny Scot'.

[4] Waxed paper negatives were loaded into their darkslides usually immediately after being blotted. Thus they were loaded damp, although clearly rarely exposed until dry. The slides were glass-fronted and wooden or slate backed. The paper was therefore held under some pressure between glass front plate and slide-back. By loading it damp, and allowing drying to take place in the slide, an absolutely flat negative was guaranteed. The tight fit of the slides ensured that little air reached the paper. Keith was indeed right in assuming that air degenerated the light sensitive emulsion.

[5] Keith was not unique in working at these hours of the day. With an admitted exposure of between four and eight minutes, early morning merely gave him time to concentrate, time to set up in peace, and to be relatively sure of passers-by not interfering with his photography.

[6] High sunlight did not suit the waxed paper process. It gave quite negative contrast and extremely bright conditions caused it to solarise – that is, partly reverse, on occasions.

[7] Modern emulsions are developed to carefully controlled negative contrasts to suit the printing papers we use. Early processes, however, could more easily be 'developed to finality' without any undesirable side-effects. Thus, the development would proceed until there was no more exposed image to develop and then it would stop. Continued immersion in the developers, while slightly increasing the risk of staining, would not usually damage the negative's printing characteristics. Some modern bromide papers exhibit similar characteristics.

[8] This particular effect was caused by the exposure being increased to just less than that required to effect a solarisation. Just before that point is reached, on the plateau of the negative's characteristic curve, there is a marked and general reduction in mid-tone/highlight contrast.

APPENDIX II

THE WAXED PAPER PROCESS

In the 1840s the most commonly used processes in photography were the French daguerreotype and the British calotype processes, the latter having been invented by William Henry Fox Talbot, the squire of Lacock in Wiltshire, in 1841. The calotype process, the first to give a negative from which multiple prints could be produced, was a milestone in the evolution of photography and, although quality was initially lower than with the daguerreotype, the increased facility the process afforded made its success inevitable.

However, the process had a number of shortcomings, the major one being the fact that the paper fibre of the negative was printed through into the positive. This was reduced somewhat by the simple expedient of waxing the paper before printing.

Basically, it was not the *actual* paper texture, but a photographic image of it in the negative, which caused the problem. The calotype was based on plain paper, and the light sensitive chemistry was absorbed by the paper. Thus the entire thickness of the paper was capable of recording a photographic image. The back of the paper therefore could, in addition to recording a photographic image of the subject, record an image of the paper fibres in front of it.

It was the simple fact of this chemical impregnation of the paper that lay at the root of the trouble. Gustave le Gray suggested that, if the paper was waxed *before it was sensitised,* then the chemicals could not be absorbed as completely into the thickness. He argued therefore that this impression of texture would be considerably reduced.

This simple answer was however not achieved straight away and le Gray experimented with several different ideas before the waxed paper process was evolved. First of all he bound the light-sensitive chemicals in albumen – white of egg – and coated that onto the paper. Next he tried collodion on paper – working along surprisingly similar lines to those which, with glass, would result in Archer and Fry's wet plate process. It is interesting to note that the le Gray collodion-on-paper process was also loaded and exposed wet.

He even tried a wet version of Talbot's calotype process, although he did not comment on what he expected to achieve. That was in 1848, the year before his waxed paper process was first published.

Le Gray was confident that the future success of photography lay with paper negatives and, in his writings, constantly urged his readers to listen to him and not follow the false prophets who advocated glass as the ideal base for photography. In his 1850 account of the Waxed Paper Process published in Britain by T & R Willats, he urged:

> 'The negative proof upon glass is, it is true, finer but I think it a false road, and it would be much more desirable to arrive at the same results with the negative on paper.'

and again:

> 'the future and extensive application of this art will doubtless be confined to the paper process, and I cannot too much engage the amateur to direct his attention and study to it.'

The process to which he particularly urged his readers to direct their study was of course his own, and the false road in question was the albumen-on-glass process which, although rather insensitive as already mentioned, was indeed capable of extremely fine detail.

By the time Thomas Keith took up the process, he was in illustrious company – many of the most eminent photographers of the day were using le Gray's process – Roger Fenton, Paul Pretsch, and many others

in Britain, Henri le Secq, le Gray himself and a host of others on the continent.

In the *Photographic Journal* for 21 January 1854 (the official journal of the Photographic Society of London) a Mr Washington Teasdale had expressed a certain surprise at the number of different versions of the new process which appeared to be in use. He published a list of eight photographers, himself included, and the chemistry which they employed. He noted with surprise that the number of chemicals used in the iodizing solution varying from as few as two to as many as eight.

' By the time Thomas Keith became involved several other publications had appeared covering the same subject. (These reports, and over twenty different versions of the process give a fascinating insight into the pioneering attitude of early photographers).

What appears to have escaped the notice of many of his contemporaries, while having been perfectly clear to Thomas Keith himself, was the simple fact that chemicals become exhausted. Many of the versions of the process to which Dr Keith would have been able to refer in the various journals of the day used minute quantities of each solution which, although entirely fresh at the outset, would quickly reach exhaustion. As he said in his speech:

> 'One must not be economical with the silver bath.'

and earlier:

> 'A great secret of success is keeping the silver bath in good order. Every sheet immersed in it removes much silver and there is a constant weakening of the bath going on. It is necessary therefore to keep making up this waste, by adding silver to it from time to time. Using so strongly iodized papers as the above, the bath soon gets exhausted and unless you leave your papers in a much longer time than 10 minutes, or else keep adding fresh silver and acetic acid you very soon find your negatives covered with white spots and patches arising from the decomposition not having thoroughly taken place, or else they come up feeble and flat . . . .'

The mere fact that such a lengthy comment, rather than a mere passing mention, was felt necessary suggests perhaps that the practise was anything but commonplace.

By thus using a very large quantity of very strong solution, and by passing only a strictly limited number of sheets of paper through it, Keith was guaranteeing for himself much higher consistency and quality. For example, while one version of the process suggested that one fluid ounce of nitrate bath containing 154 grains of silver nitrate was all that was required for an unspecified number of negatives, Keith insisted on twelve fluid ounces containing 360 grains for a maximum of twelve negatives. Although his bath was a little weaker in terms of nitrate per fluid ounce, the greater volume of solution meant less oxidation and greater consistency over the period of immersion. The precision of Keith's work was the key to his success. For others, unaware of the chemical considerations, failure must have been much more common.

For that first version of the iodising solution, put forward by Joseph Sidebottom of Manchester, an immersion of two hours was suggested in that small amount of strong solution, while Keith recommended overnight immersion of his twelve sheets. This too led to greater consistency from batch to batch.

It should be stressed that many of the chemicals which found their way into later (1852-6) versions of the process were not included in le Gray's original treatise. Even Dr Keith added two chemicals to the le Gray recipe – potassium bromide and common salt. Le Gray's original iodising solution contained potassium iodide, sugar of milk, potassium cyanide and potassium fluoride. Keith, no doubt acutely aware of the risks involved in their use, quickly abandoned the cyanide and the fluoride. He also substituted plain distilled water for the 'rice water plus isinglass' of the original recipe. The removal of the isinglass is interesting, as it, in conjunction with the rice water, was the binding material which made the chemistry more of an emulsion and less like the absorbed chemistry of the calotype.

The main difference between the Keith and le Gray versions, apart from the absence of the chemicals already mentioned, were in the strengths of the solutions employed. As he said at the beginning of his speech:

> 'I began with Le Gray's weak solutions but soon found it impossible to get anything like a decent negative with an exposure of under 30 or 40 minutes.'

What he was actually achieving was a higher 'speed', an all-important increase in sensitivity, essential for the climate in which he was working. This is reflected in the fact that, while Mr Sidebottom's process required an exposure of 10 minutes, Keith was achieving considerable success with much shorter times. Although he mentions in his paper that his exposure range was from two to eight minutes, there is clear evidence from many of his finest images that he was working more usually with the shorter rather than the longer exposures. Views such as those in White Horse Close, High School Wynd, the Grassmarket, and at Inverkeithing which include figures and animals suggest exposures of between one and two minutes.

In fact in views such as 'North side of the Lawnmarket' the movement of horses suggests that an exposure of less than a minute is likely. There are also a number of occasions where what must surely be casual passers-by are recorded with relative clarity.

His camera was probably of the folding bellows type with a cross-section of approximately 12″ × 12″. Within that square frame size he could produce both his vertical and horizontal pictures. The camera seen in the stereoscopic view of the group of photographers at Craigmillar has been carefully measured in a large enlargement and, in relation to the length of a man's arm, is approximately the right size to have produced negatives of the dimensions of Thomas Keith's.

The fact that the darkslide would, like the camera back, have been square would pose no problem. The paper, cut to size, would have been held in place along two opposite edges by the edges of the frame of the slide while thin tapes held the open edges against the backplate of the slide. The front cover glass would then be clamped into place to hold the entire assembly rigid and flat.

REFERENCES

Introduction

1 A. L. Coburn 'Old Masters of Photography' *Century Magazine* Oct 1915.
2 John Gray *Calotypes by D O Hill and Robert Adamson selected from his collection by Andrew Elliot* published privately 1928 (written 1885).
3 Neven du Mont 'The Camera was a Curiosity' in *Picturing Today* 1950.

Chapter 2

1 Appendix I p 81.
2 Appendix II p 84.
3 Appendix I p 81.
4 Appendix I p 81.

Chapter 3

1 After a short time the association with *Photographic Notes* ended and, again briefly, the journal published the proceedings of the Birmingham Photographic Society and other provincial groups.
2 Appendix I p 81.
3 *The Pencil of Nature* was originally intended as a ten-part work, containing a total of fifty calotypes. Talbot never got round to completing it on such a scale. Apart from a small private memorial publication entitled *Record of the deathbed of CMW*, published in the spring of 1844, *Pencil of Nature* was the first photographically-illustrated book. It was certainly the first to go on public sale and part one appeared in June 1844. In all, six parts were published over the next few months, at no set interval from each other, and about twenty-four calotypes were issued. The pictures in the book were of course pasted-in photographic prints. In 1845 Talbot published *Sun Pictures in Scotland* – containing twenty-three plates of views and buildings which would in later years become favourite haunts of Scotland's photographers.

Thus by 1845 the calotype had already proved its worth in several fields. The daguerreotype was of course entirely unsuited to use in this way. Further to the associations between the Keith family and the pioneering uses of photography, it is, however, interesting to note that *Evidence of the Truth of the Christian Religion*, 1848, by Alexander Keith, was the first book in the world to have illustrations based on daguerreotypes (taken by George Skene Keith).

BIBLIOGRAPHY

C. S. Minto. *Thomas Keith: Photographer*. Edinburgh City Libraries 1966.

D. B. Thomas. *The Science Museum Photography Collection*. HMSO 1969.

Rev Alexander Keith. *Evidence of the Truth of the Christian Religion*. W. Whyte & Co. 1848.

David Bruce. *The Sun Pictures*. Studio Vista 1971.

Roy Strong/Colin Ford. *The Hill Adamson Calotypes*. Times Newspapers 1971.

Aaron Scharf. *Pioneers of Photography*. BBC Publication 1975.

R. O. Dougan. *The Scottish Tradition in Photography*. Saltire Society 1948.

William Lake Price. *A Manual of Photographic Manipulation*. 1859.

Sir David Brewster. *The Stereoscope, its Theory, History and Construction*. 1971 reprint of 1856 edition, Morgan & Morgan, New York.

Gustave le Gray. *A Practical Treatise on photography on Paper and Glass*. T. & R. Willats, London 1850.

Christopher Hibbert. *ILN Social History of Victorian Britain*. Angus and Robertson 1975.

Dorothy Marshall. *The Life and Times of Queen Victoria*. Weidenfeld & Nicholson/Book Club Associates 1972.

H. J. P. Arnold. *William Henry Fox Talbot, Pioneer of Photography and Man of Science*. Hutchinson/Benham 1977.

Photographic Notes 1856.

The Photographic Journal 1854-6.

Century Magazine 1915.

Photo World 1950.

The Illustrated London News 1853-7.

The Scottish Medical Journal.

The Lancet.

INDEX